D0434543

The End of
Macro-Economics?

DAVID SIMPSON

Economist, The Standard Life Assurance Company
Professor of Economics, University of Strathclyde, 1975-88

Published by
INSTITUTE OF ECONOMIC AFFAIRS
1994

First published in October 1994

by

THE INSTITUTE OF ECONOMIC AFFAIRS
2 Lord North Street, Westminster,
London SW1P 3LB

Hobart Paper 126

ISSN 0073-2818

ISBN 0-255 36338-9

Cover design by David Lucas

Printed in Great Britain by
BOURNE PRESS LIMITED, BOURNEMOUTH, DORSET
Set in Baskerville Roman 11 on 12 point

CONTENTS

[3]

FOREWORD

In 1973, the Institute published a paper by Ludwig Lachmann,[1] the implications of which were described in the Editor's Preface as 'revolutionary'. Lachmann argued that economics had taken a wrong turn, relying too much on the analysis of macro-economic aggregates and losing sight of the subject's micro-economic foundations. In his words, 'Macro-economic theories without micro-economic substructure are bound to rest upon rather hollow foundations'. Lachmann criticised some of the favoured macro-economic remedies of the 1970s (such as incomes policies) as depriving '...the market of its main function'.

Twenty years on, in *Hobart Paper* No.126, Professor David Simpson takes up Lachmann's theme, arguing that many economists are still set on the wrong course and that there is an undue emphasis on macro-economic thinking. From his opening paragraph, Professor Simpson's message is clear:

> 'The essential distinguishing feature of the developed market economy is incessant qualitative change...Aggregate concepts such as the natural rate of unemployment and the total quantity of money obscure rather than clarify thinking about the market economy.' (p.9)

In his *Hobart Paper*, Simpson examines the origins of macro-economics (Section II), explaining that in the post-war period it was embraced by a large part of the economics profession with the notable exception of the 'Austrians'. He then analyses (Sections III and IV) the record of macro-economic policy. In his view it has failed: '...aggregate concepts have led to muddled thinking and thus to unsuccessful and even harmful policies' (p.16). He is particularly concerned that governments have been misled by macro-economic forecasting models (which have generally performed poorly). In his view, though 'pattern predictions' are feasible, it is not possible to

---

[1] L.M. Lachmann, *Macro-economic Thinking and the Market Economy*, Hobart Paper No. 56, London: Institute of Economic Affairs, first published August 1973.

produce '...acceptable numerical forecasts of future events using macro-economic models' (p.31).

Section IV discusses reasons for the failure of policies based on macro-economic thinking and considers some recent developments in macro-economic theorising (for instance, in the theory of economic growth). Professor Simpson contends that new growth theory '...has no original insights of its own to contribute. All it does is try to squeeze the intuition of earlier "literary" economists into a mathematical straitjacket' (p.48); macro-theory in general has, in Simpson's words, gone down a '...*cul-de-sac* of increasing formalism and heightened levels of abstraction' (p.49).

By contrast, the 'classical alternative' (Sections V and VI) emphasises '...the importance of uncertainty, innovation, entrepreneurship and institutional evolution, and avoids spurious precision' (p.76). It has quite different policy implications. Professor Simpson points, for example, to Hayekian ideas about deregulated banking and suggests that '...the anomaly of attempted state control of the money supply may not last much longer' (p.60), even though he acknowledges that view may as yet be too radical to be politically acceptable.

Professor Simpson's clearly expressed and thoughtful views, with their strong Austrian overtones and their hard-hitting criticisms of macro-economics, will undoubtedly provoke controversy. Authors of *Hobart Papers* have never shrunk from expressing radical views, no matter how politically unacceptable they may have seemed at the time: Professor Simpson's paper follows in that tradition. The opinions expressed in *Hobart Paper* No.126 are, of course, those of the author, not of the IEA (which has no corporate view), its Trustees, Directors or Advisers.

October 1994   COLIN ROBINSON
Editorial Director, Institute of Economic Affairs;
Professor of Economics, University of Surrey

THE AUTHOR

DAVID SIMPSON was educated at the Universities of Edinburgh and Harvard, and then worked for the Statistical Office of the United Nations in New York. From 1975 to 1988 he was Professor of Economics at the University of Strathclyde. He is now the Economist at The Standard Life Assurance Company, an Honorary Professor at Heriot-Watt University, Edinburgh, and a member of the IEA's academic advisory council.

Professor Simpson's published writings include several books: *Problems of Input-Output Tables and Analysis* (1966); *General Equilibrium Analysis* (1975); and *The Political Economy of Growth* (1983); and articles in journals ranging from *Econometrica* to *Scientific American*.

ACKNOWLEDGEMENTS

It has been my good fortune to have learned economics from, amongst others, four inspiring teachers: Alexander Gray, Alan Peacock, Gottfried Haberler, and Wassily Leontief. Although each came from quite different traditions in economic thought and none can be held responsible for the views expressed in this paper, I do not believe that any of them would strongly disagree with those views.

Professor Edith Penrose and Sir Alan Peacock kindly read an earlier draft of this paper. I am grateful to them for their comments, as I am to two anonymous referees and to Professor Colin Robinson for his unfailing encouragement. Sharon Macdonald, Lesley Moffat and Joyce McLean patiently produced many revised drafts as well as the final text.

D.S.

I. INTRODUCTION

The essential distinguishing feature of the developed market economy is incessant qualitative change; new consumer and capital goods, new methods of production and distribution, new forms of organisation and new markets are continuously being created and old ones destroyed.[1] This essential feature is obscured by a macro-economic perspective. Aggregate concepts such as the natural rate of unemployment and the total quantity of money obscure rather than clarify thinking about the market economy.

Macro-economics is a method of economic analysis developed mainly after the Second World War with the objective of stabilising economy-wide fluctuations in output and employment and promoting economic growth in market economies. Its development was determined by the needs of policy rather than theory. Cycles of prosperity and recession, of inflation and deflation, had been objects of study since economic thought began, but macro-economics represented a new approach to these topics.

The principal features of the new method were an exclusive reliance on aggregates and averages, the exclusion of all non-quantifiable data, and the application to the evolving historical data of methods derived from the natural sciences, especially from physics. It asserted the stability of empirically observed relationships, and tried to estimate numerical values for their parameters.

Proponents of these methods believed that by the use of mathematical 'models' of each national economy, they could forecast the future path of the principal economic aggregates, and thereby identify the appropriate policies required to achieve the objectives of full employment, steady growth and price stability.

After almost half a century of experience of applying macro-economic methods in the developed market economies, the

---

[1] J.A. Schumpeter, *Capitalism, Socialism and Democracy*, London: Allen & Unwin, 1976, Ch.7.

first two of these objectives have been discarded as unattainable by macro-economic policy. So far as price stability is concerned, no way has yet been found to achieve it in a manner compatible with sustained economic growth. As a distinguished macro-economist has said of the UK experience:

> 'It is necessary to note that over the past two decades the UK has tried almost every macro-economic strategy, and has failed at each. The credibility of UK macro-economic policy making is largely non-existent.'[2]

Given the duration and varied circumstances of these experiments, the failures of macro-economic policy are most likely attributable to the inadequacy of the underlying theory. The defects of macro-economic theory can be divided into three classes. There is, *first*, formalism, meaning the inappropriate use of concepts outside their original context. *Second*, macro-economics abstracts from essential features of the market economy. *Third*, macro-economics assumes that the algebraic sum of the elements of an aggregate is all that matters; the effects of changes in its composition are irrelevant.

In the next section of this paper the nature and origins of macro-economic theory are discussed. Section III discusses the failures of macro-economic policy when applied to such issues as full employment, economic growth and price stability in the context of the British economy. Section IV shows why theory is unsatisfactory and how it has contributed to policy failure.

Section V sets out the elements of an alternative, classical, approach to understanding fluctuations and growth. The key element of this approach is the recognition that a market economy is primarily a network of relationships between human beings. Each individual's perception of economic activity is fragmentary and incomplete; *all* economic behaviour therefore has something of an entrepreneurial character. Market economies are characterised by continuing evolutionary change, so that present and future phenomena are qualitatively different from those of the past. A full range of factors (not just those which are readily quantifiable) is encompassed in this approach; it is multi-faceted and disaggregated.

---

[2] D.A. Currie, 'Economic Viewpoint', in *Economic Outlook*, London Business School, Vol. 17, No. 5, February 1993, p.34.

When it is applied to the contemporary market economy the classical approach leads to rather different conclusions from those suggested by macro-economics. The implications for government policy, for business and for academic teaching and research are spelled out in Section VI, while conclusions are drawn in Section VII.

II. WHAT IS MACRO-ECONOMICS?

What Macro-economics is About

Macro-economics is about economy-wide fluctuations in output, employment and prices. Until the Second World War these phenomena were usually studied by economists under the heading of Business Cycles. After the war, however, 'Business Cycles' was displaced from the Economics syllabus in universities throughout the Western world by something called 'Macro-economics'. This was the name given to the new body of theory, originating with Keynes, which purported to show the proximate causes of fluctuations in employment in developed economies and how they could be avoided. A novel aspect of this theory was that its elements consisted exclusively of aggregates, such as total (national) output, total (national) investment, etc., and averages, such as the price level. It is the method of thinking only in terms of aggregates and averages which characterises macro-economics and distinguishes it from earlier analyses of fluctuations in output, prices and employment.

The introduction of macro-economics coincided with an increasing formalisation of method in economics, so that from the beginning it depended on the application of mathematical methods derived from the natural sciences, and the crowding-out of non-quantifiable factors. Thus macro-economics represented a discontinuity in its method of approach to the issues it addressed. From the beginning it was policy-driven, and depended on empirically based correlations between aggregates. As compared to micro-economics, the theory of value, where the chain of reasoning stretches back in an unbroken line to the 16th century, macro-economics has been characterised by an *ad hoc* approach, despite attempts to give it a more secure theoretical foundation.

The Origins of Macro-economics

While antecedents can be found for thinking in aggregate terms,[1] the origins of contemporary macro-economics can be

---

[1] See, for example, W.J. Baumol, *Economic Dynamics*, New York: Macmillan, 1951,

 [*cont'd p.13*]

traced to Keynes's *General Theory*.[2] Keynes was a man of intellectual distinction and sensitivity, with wide-ranging interests and abilities encompassing the arts as well as philosophy and mathematics.[3] Most importantly, he had worked in the Treasury during the First World War, helping to manage the government's finances. He knew from first-hand experience as speculator, trader and insurance company chairman how the London financial and commodity markets worked. Keynes also had some experience of estate management and farming. From the early 1920s until his death in 1946, perhaps no other person had a better understanding of how the British economy worked. This understanding bore fruit in his handling of government finances during the Second World War, which may eventually come to be regarded as his finest achievement.

Despite his great intellectual abilities, Keynes's understanding of the economy was intuitive. Although the author of a number of books, and editor of the *Economic Journal*, Keynes was never an economic theorist. Like most great books on economics, his *General Theory* is a terrible muddle, through which shines his frustration with the orthodox economic doctrine of his time – a doctrine which held unquestioned sway over government economic policy between the Wars.

Throughout the 1920s and 1930s, Keynes could not disguise his impatience with conventional opinion, using every opportunity to ridicule it. He was thus widely regarded as 'unsound'. His intuitive view was that there must be something wrong with the working of an economic system which produced sustained unemployment of resources in the middle of unsatisfied wants. The orthodox view, supported by neo-classical theory, was that government intervention could only make things worse. Keynes realised that in order to change economic policy it was not enough to point out the inadequacies of the neo-classical theory. To get his ideas put into practice, he had first to replace the prevailing theory with

Part I. See also Section IV below (subsection entitled 'Conclusions', p.49). An earlier example is Quesnay's *Tableau Economique*.

[2] J.M. Keynes, *The General Theory of Employment, Interest, and Money*, London: Macmillan, 1936.

[3] R. Skidelsky, *John Maynard Keynes*, Vol.Two: *The Economist as Saviour, 1920-1937*, London: Macmillan, 1992.

a more acceptable one. As its title suggests, this was his intention in writing the *General Theory*.

Keynes had a practical man's understandable fondness for thinking in aggregate terms. Most of the aggregate variables which became a familiar part of post-war macro-economic theory first appear in the *General Theory*. However, the book also laid emphasis on a number of other elements, such as the state of expectations, which were not always carried over into macro-economics.

What his famous book failed to do was to provide a coherent and consistent alternative to neo-classical theory. A year later, Hicks provided just such an interpretation of the General Theory, within an analytical framework which could also be used to represent the neo-classical orthodoxy.[4] This framework, the IS-LM diagram, became the basis of macro-economic theory for 30 years after the War. So-called 'Keynesians' and 'Monetarists', whose sectarian disputes in the 1970s and 1980s did so much to bring economics as a discipline into disrepute, both share this common approach.

Universal Adoption of Macro-Economics (Except for the 'Austrians')

Although it was later to become fashionable for 'Keynesian' economists to be identified with criticisms of the shortcomings of a market economy, while neo-classical macro-economists were identified with a belief in its efficacious working, it is important to underline that in the post-war period macro-economic thinking was embraced by almost all shades of political opinion within the profession. Only the 'Austrians' consistently rejected macro-economic thinking. Despite their sometimes similar political views, neo-classical and Austrian economists stand at opposite ends of the methodological spectrum.[5]

Hicks's success was largely because he turned phenomena characterised by dynamic and out-of-equilibrium behaviour into the familiar paradigm of comparative statics – a static and equilibrium method of analysis – thus preserving methodo-

---

[4] J.R. Hicks, 'Mr Keynes and the Classics', *Econometrica*, 1937.

[5] 'Hardly an author can be found, not even Keynes himself, who is so much the exact antipode of Milton Friedman in every part of the economist's theoretical vision as Carl Menger.' (Erich Streissler in J.R. Hicks and W. Weber (eds.), *Carl Menger and the Austrian School of Economics*, London: Macmillan, 1973, p.165.)

logical unity with the orthodox neo-classical theory. Since both the neo-classical and the 'Keynesian' views of the workings of the aggregate economy could be exhibited within a single framework, it was instantly adopted by most of the academic profession. In the post-war consensual division of labour, price and output phenomena relating to the long term (the trend) were to be the preserve of micro-economic theory (the new name for the theory of value). This showed how quantities and relative prices were determined in a market economy. Macro-economics was to be the new complementary discipline which explained economy-wide fluctuations around the trend – that is, the cycle. There was an implicit acceptance of the separability of growth and cycle.

Keynes lived for 10 years after the publication of his *General Theory*. Although he never formally endorsed Hicks's interpretation, he did not disavow it, even though it omitted key elements of his work. It may be he realised that Hicks's interpretation provided him with just the theoretical battering ram he required for his policy prescriptions to be accepted.

The essential message of the *General Theory* was that, left to itself, a market economy would settle down for prolonged periods at an aggregate equilibrium which fell short of full employment. It was therefore the function of government, by appropriately stimulating aggregate demand, to restore aggregate output to a full employment level. In this way, said Hayek later, Keynes and his disciples lent scientific authority to 'the age-old superstition that by increasing the aggregate of money expenditure we can lastingly ensure prosperity and full employment'.[6]

---

[6] F.A. Hayek, *New Studies in Philosophy, Politics, Economics and the History of Ideas*, London: Routledge & Kegan Paul, 1978, p.218.

III. THE FAILURE OF
MACRO-ECONOMIC POLICY

Introduction

Just as the overall macro-economic perspective misses the whole point of the market economy, aggregate concepts have led to muddled thinking and thus to unsuccessful and even harmful policies.

For example, there is the concept of 'the quantity of money'. Strictly speaking, there is no such thing as *the* quantity of money. It is simply incorrect to regard different classes of financial asset as if they were perfect substitutes for each other, quite apart from the question of multiple currencies. This mistaken belief is largely responsible for the unsuccessful attempt by central banks to fine-tune bank lending.

Then there is the concept of the 'output gap', commonly used by City analysts as a determinant of the rate of inflation. It is supposed to represent the gap between aggregate output and aggregate productive capacity. The wide divergence of estimates of the size of this gap, ranging in the first quarter of 1994 from 1·5 per cent (Goldman Sachs) to 7 per cent (Bank of England),[1] points to the underlying conceptual unreality of such aggregates which take no account of mismatches between capacity and demand in individual firms or industries.

Another measure of aggregate capacity which is popular with macro-economists is the (purely hypothetical) minimum rate of unemployment consistent with non-accelerating inflation (NAIRU).[2] This is a concept without any counterpart in reality. Not surprisingly, econometric estimates reported by the Bank of England range from 1 million to 2·8 million.[3]

---

[1] S.Brittan, 'The Enigma of the UK Output Gap', *Financial Times*, 14 February 1994.

[2] M. Friedman, 'The Role of Monetary Policy', *American Economic Review*, Vol. 58, no. 1, 1968, pp.1-17; also Friedman, *The Counter-Revolution in Monetary Theory*, IEA Occasional Paper No. 33, 1970, and *Unemployment versus Inflation?*, IEA Occasional Paper No. 44, 1975, London: Institute of Economic Affairs.

[3] S.Brittan, *op.cit.*

Another aggregate concept is that of 'Competitiveness'. When applied to a country or continent it is difficult to give this concept any meaning, other than in the special case where a country suffers at the same time a fixed and over-valued exchange rate. It is misleading principally because it implies that a country's benefit from international trade arises from its exports rather than from its imports. The confusion of thought induced by the false analogy of competition between firms and competition between countries has led to neo-protectionist trade policies, and to the support of public subsidies for manufacturing at the expense of services.[4]

All these concepts suffer from the theoretical flaws discussed in Section IV below. First, however, we turn to the macro-economic policies which have been so unsuccessfully pursued since the War.

Macro-economic Policy Since the War

Macro-economic policy was applied in the developed market economies after the Second World War to achieve the following objectives:

O Sustained growth (i.e. full capacity utilisation, and a smoothing out of the business cycle about a rising trend).

O Full employment.

O Price stability.

Following the Keynesian revolution, it was believed that these objectives were within the responsibility of government to deliver, and within the capability of government to achieve by the application of appropriate fiscal and monetary policies. Subsequently, the principal objective of economic policy swung from full employment to the achievement of price stability.

In the early post-war period, the principal concern was to avert a repetition of the levels of unemployment which had been a feature of the 1920s and 1930s. Keynes's diagnosis had been that unemployment was a consequence of a deficiency of

---

[4] See P.Krugman, *Peddling Prosperity*, New York: W. W. Norton, 1994, Ch.10.

aggregate demand, which it was within the power of government to correct. The instrument by which this end was to be achieved was the management of aggregate demand through discretionary fiscal policy. Under the influence of pre-war experience, the possibility of sustained inflation was generally disregarded. In any case, inflation was thought to be amenable to the same techniques of aggregate demand management as unemployment. The existence of unemployment indicated an insufficiency of aggregate demand, while inflation indicated too much. Full employment at stable prices was thought to be attainable.

Historically Low Unemployment

At first, the policy of demand management appeared to work, at least so far as the principal objective of full employment was concerned. For some 30 years after 1945, unemployment rates were at historically low levels in most of the developed economies, and recessions were so mild and infrequent as to be almost unnoticeable. The mildness of these recessions in the early post-war period, compared to pre-war periods, can be seen with hindsight to have been due in large part to the significantly increased share of the public sector in economic activity, together with the automatically counter-cyclical nature of much of that activity.

On the other hand, discretionary counter-cyclical fiscal policies, as envisaged by macro-economic theory, proved to be ineffective in practice – even destabilising – because of the problem of lags (diagnostic, policy and operational) between the perception of the need for such measures and their effects. In order to avoid the destabilising effects of, for example, increasing aggregate demand after a recession is over, expansionary measures should be implemented well in advance of a cyclical upturn. But, as we shall see, turning points in the cycle are precisely what macro-economic forecasts have not been able to predict.

The apparent disregard which Keynes had shown for the possible dangers of inflation appeared to be justified by the events of the 1950s and 1960s. In Britain, the rate of inflation averaged less than 4 per cent; when it did rise above 5 per cent in 1969, that was the first time for 14 years. Whenever inflation did threaten, collective wage bargaining was usually blamed, and statutory control of incomes was periodically imposed.[5]

End of Post-War Consensus

The post-war consensus was brought to an abrupt end in the early 1970s by the co-existence of rising inflation and rising unemployment. The fundamental Keynesian doctrine that a government could spend its way out of a recession was publicly rejected in 1976 by the then Prime Minister, Mr James (now Lord) Callaghan, at the Labour Party Conference of that year.

By the end of the 1970s a new macro-economic consensus had emerged. Instead of using macro-economic policy (mainly fiscal) to promote growth of output and hence employment, while using micro-economic policy (incomes policies) to hold down inflation, the new consensus suggested the reverse. The Government should direct its macro-economic policy instructions (this time mainly monetary) towards the control of inflation, whilst relying on micro-economic policies (tax and labour market reforms) to improve the performance of the economy in terms of growth and employment.

Behind this change of policy instruments there lay a change of priority in policy objectives: price stability was to be given priority over full employment. The reversal of priorities was justified with the argument that the achievement of price stability was a prerequisite of the sustained growth of employment. While there might be a phase of high unemployment in the transition to price stability, in the long run there was no trade-off between unemployment and inflation. Furthermore, it was argued that inflation (the absence of price stability) was a phenomenon which had exclusively monetary origins, and therefore was capable of being controlled through the adoption of the appropriate monetary policies.

While it was recognised that the transition to an era of price stability might involve a short period of painful adjustment, it seemed to be believed that once expectations of future inflation had been revised downwards, unrealistic wage demands would abate and a period of sustained economic

---

[5] See F. Blackaby (ed.), *British Economic Policy 1960-74*, Cambridge: Cambridge University Press, 1978.

growth would be ushered in. Any remaining unemployment in this latter period would reflect only inflexible labour markets, which could be addressed by specific labour market policies. There was a tacit admission that full employment was no longer a major priority of government policy. Like economic growth and the balance of payments, it could be left to market forces.

Thus the Conservative Government which took office in 1979 embarked on an economic policy which explicitly reversed the priorities and instruments of earlier post-war governments. Whereas previously the principal objective of government economic policy had been to secure full employment, while price stability was left to market forces, with the occasional assistance of *ad hoc* statutory controls, now the principal objective of macro-economic policy was to be the achievement of price stability, with the realisation of full employment left to market forces.

Once again, this policy at first seemed to work. After a brief but deep recession (the 'painful adjustment'), the British economy grew rapidly for some nine years from March 1981. By 1986, price stability seemed to have been attained, and if full employment had not been realised, at least unemployment had been falling for three successive years.

Once again these hopes were disappointed, as the inflationary boom of 1988-90 was followed by the recession of 1990-92. Following the withdrawal of the pound from the ERM in September 1992, the Government announced a numerical target for price stability, but significantly no corresponding target for unemployment. No indication has been given as to how the inflation target is to be achieved, nor of whether full employment is an objective of policy, and, if it is, what policy instruments might be used for its attainment.

Half a century on, two of the three traditional objectives of macro-economic policy have been recognised to be beyond the scope of that policy. Insofar as government can contribute to their realisation, it will not be through macro-economic policies. The third objective, price stability, is still believed to be within the power of government to achieve, in particular through the operation of monetary policy. Two problems remain.

First, in monetary policy, there has recently been a shift from targeting intermediate variables such as monetary aggregates or market interest rates to targeting the ultimate objective itself. This suggests a loss of belief in the stability of macro-economic relationships, and perhaps a belated awareness of the uncertainties and lags in the impact of monetary policy measures.

Second, ultimate variables such as indices of retail prices are subject to numerous forces outside the control of the monetary authorities, including domestic fiscal policy and foreign fiscal and monetary policies. The globalisation of economic activity, in particular of capital markets, has reduced significantly the degrees of freedom of national governments.

In some other countries – such as France during the 1980s – attempts to achieve price stability through monetary policy have been realised, but at the apparent cost of low growth and increasing unemployment. For most contemporary developed market economies, the combination of sustained growth of output with price stability appears to remain as elusive an objective as ever.

Unemployment Unexplained

Contemporary macro-economics began with Keynes's attempts to understand the causes of the unemployment he observed in the 1920s and 1930s. Proponents of the 'new' macro-economics have said their theory should be judged by the extent to which it proves useful to applied economists. It might therefore be reasonable to suppose that macro-economics can cast some light on the causes of contemporary unemployment. In fact, while opinion is divided on the appropriate remedies for the levels of unemployment currently observed in the developed economies, it is generally agreed that these remedies do not include active macro-economic management.[6]

The orthodox Keynesian view that full employment could be realised simply by appropriate government management of

---

[6] See, for example, OECD, *Jobs Study*, June 1994, OECD, *Employment Outlook*, July 1994, and the Papers prepared for the TUC Full Employment Conference, London, 5 July 1994.

aggregate national expenditure *via* fiscal policy has long been abandoned. The other major macro-economic approach, monetarism, suggested that appropriate management of national aggregate expenditure *via* monetary policy, together with the operation of market forces, would be sufficient to realise full employment. This view has also been discredited by events.

It is now widely recognised that the trend of unemployment throughout the developed market economies (which can be identified with the 26 member-states of the OECD) has been getting worse since 1960. In any particular economy, at any moment of time, unemployment appears to be higher than at the corresponding point in the previous cycle.

The total number out of work in the OECD countries at the present time is about 33 million, at an average rate of 8·0 per cent of the workforce. In the European Union, about 18 million people are defined as unemployed, at a cost to member-state governments estimated at some £150 billion in 1993. In the UK, the number of unemployed is about 2·6 million, or 9.2 per cent of the workforce.

Aggregate Explanations for Unemployment (Continued)

Undeterred by their previous failures, macro-economists have continued to put forward explanations for unemployment based on their perspective of the national economy and the labour force as being aggregate entities of unchanging composition.

One of these is that unemployment is to be explained by real wages being too high. While it is easy to see the meaning of such an explanation in the context of a firm or even an industry, the attempt to explain *aggregate* unemployment by the level of the *average* wage in the nation as a whole is difficult to understand. Yet, together with average aggregate labour productivity, these concepts are regularly featured in discourses in the financial press, in government publications[7] and even among economists employed in the City of London.

---

[7] For example, in January 1985 the Treasury published a Yellow Paper which concluded that a change of 1 per cent in average real wages could be associated with a change in the opposite direction in aggregate employment of between one-half and 1 per cent.

The kind of confusion to which this type of macro-economic thinking can lead is shown when politicians[8] and journalists begin to exhort businessmen to restrict the wage increases granted by their firms to some aggregate norm, determined by some notional movement in aggregate productivity. The key flaw in this macro-economic explanation of unemployment is revealed by the question: Why would the employers be willing to pay more than they can afford? No satisfactory answer to this question has been forthcoming from the macro-economists, although various attempts have been made.

For instance, it has frequently been alleged that it is the attempt by trade unions to obtain 'excessive' real wages that is responsible for high unemployment. Since the bargaining power of trade unions has visibly diminished throughout the Western world, and particularly in the UK, in the course of the 1980s, this explanation can hardly account for increasing levels of unemployment.

'Disenchantment' with Macro-Economic Thinking

Throughout the last decade there has been a growing disenchantment with macro-economic thinking about unemployment.

'The issue is too often presented in Treasury documents and elsewhere in terms of broad national averages. But the demand for labour depends as much upon relative as on average real wages. Pay did not adjust sufficiently to occupational, sectoral and regional differences in the supply and demand for work. The long-standing preference among trade unions for centralised pay bargaining and nation-wide rates of pay is one reason why heavy unemployment in some areas during the 1980s coincided with labour shortages, particularly of skilled labour, in others.'[9]

In other words, useful explanations of unemployment must recognise the need for disaggregation: different factors account for variations in the rate of unemployment amongst

---

[8] 'As the 1980s wore on, I became more and more convinced that employers rather than unions were responsible for pay settlements incompatible with high employment.' (N. Lawson, *The View From Number Eleven*, London: Bantam Press, 1993, p.432.)

[9] N. Lawson, *ibid.*, p.431.

groups categorised by duration of unemployment, by locality, by age, by sex and by skill. Only when these differences are recognised is there the possibility of understanding the causes of unemployment.

Furthermore, aggregate unemployment rates, which are the staple diet of macro-economics, disguise important underlying shifts in the pattern of employment.[10] Over the last quarter of a century, new technology and other innovations have eliminated what were relatively well-paid jobs for unskilled men in industry in the developed market economies, while most of the unskilled jobs which have been created in the same period have been in the services sector, relatively low paid, often part-time, and usually taken by women. At the same time there has been an increase in the demand for skilled workers.

Since 1977, employment for men in the UK has fallen by 2·5 million, or 19 per cent, while the number of women in employment has increased by 1·3 million, or 14 per cent. Much of this new employment has been in the services sector (shops, tourism, financial services, the professions), with two-thirds involving part-time employment. By 1990, part-time work accounted for 21·8 per cent of total employment.

Survey evidence indicates that a majority of non-employed men (those who are 'economically inactive' as well as those who are registered unemployed) would prefer full-time and permanent jobs, typically high-paying work in manufacturing industry demanding job-related skills rather than educational qualifications. There therefore appears to be a mismatch between the types of jobs being created and the willingness either of men to take them or of employers to give them.

Of course, there is nothing new about this process, except for the particulars. The growth of the market economy has always meant that new jobs created might be in different industries, different regions, require different aptitudes and skills, and pay different wages from those which were lost. Macro-economics can make no contribution either to an understanding of this problem or to its solutions, since it

---

10 According to the OECD *Employment Outlook*, July 1994, in most countries about 80 per cent of job turnover (the sum of jobs created and jobs lost) is not related to the business cycle, and most turnover is due to labour displacement within industries rather than across industries.

assumes away this 'mismatch' aspect of unemployment right from the start. Yet it is precisely to this issue of job immobility that training and other contemporary labour market policies are rightly directed.

Developments in Monetary Policy

The idea of a quantifiable link between the quantity of money and the price level underpinned the medium-term financial strategy proposed by the incoming Conservative Government in 1979. This set target values for the growth rate of various measures of the money supply, with the object of bringing down the rate of inflation. Although the rate of inflation did fall, the monetary targets were seldom achieved, and were finally abandoned in 1987 and replaced with an exchange rate target. When this target, too, was abandoned, with sterling's departure from the ERM, it was replaced by a target stated in terms of an index of retail prices. It was said to be the official objective of monetary policy henceforth that this target should lie in the range of 1 to 4 per cent per annum, and that by 1997 (the end of the current Parliament) the rate of inflation should be within the lower half of this range.

But this is to target the *objective* of policy, rather than an instrument such as the money supply or the exchange rate. By so doing, it is implied that policy will be determined pragmatically; thus there is a theoretical vacuum at the heart of monetary policy-making.

A further problem is also raised. Because monetary policies operate with a time-lag, it will be necessary to forecast future inflation in order to adjust current policy. A decision by the authorities to adjust monetary policy now will depend upon a forecast (implicit or explicit) that inflation will stray outside its target range in future.

We have thus returned to a key rôle for forecasting in macro-economic policy. This time, however, it is inflation, not output or employment, which is the objective of the forecasts. But if, as we shall see in the next section, macro-economic forecasting has failed to predict changes in prices in the past, there is no reason to believe it will do any better in the future.

Although the policy time-lag may be less important in the case of monetary than of fiscal policy because the monetary authorities can act promptly, there are still lags in all the stages between the adoption of monetary measures and the impact of these on the volume of actual expenditure. Experience suggest that these lags are long and unpredictable.[11] When all of these factors are taken into account, it is not surprising that the allegedly predictable long-term relationship between the aggregate money stock and aggregate nominal income appears to have fallen apart.

Central Bank Instruments for Price Stability

How, then, do central banks attempt to achieve price stability through monetary policy?

In the USA it appears[12] that the central bank operates according to two unpublished rules: it will raise short-term interest rates if real economic growth appears likely to exceed the annual rate it regards as sustainable; and it will also raise them if inflation shows any sign of rising above the current level of just under 3 per cent. The policy of the Bank of England is currently based on a projection of where the rate of inflation will be in two years' time. The Bundesbank continues to target a wide measure of money, but is prepared to override it. While these guidelines may be an improvement on direct political control, it is not at all clear that they will result in a stable price level.

Whenever the monetary authorities have tried to fix on any definition of the aggregate stock of money (one or a whole row of Ms), either as an instrument or a target of policy, they have generally failed to achieve the stated objective. This proposition is famously embodied in Goodhart's Law.[13]

Apart from the unpredictability of individual behaviour, there may be two reasons why the monetary authorities in the developed market economies have failed: financial innovation and the loosening of controls on the international movement of capital. Money can move across borders as well as change its

---

[11] S. Dale and A.G. Haldane, 'Interest Rates and the Channels of Monetary Transmission', *Working Paper Series* No.18, Bank of England, 1993, p.34.

[12] Samuel Brittan, 'The Zenith of the Central Banks', *Financial Times*, 9 June 1994.

[13] Named after Professor Charles Goodhart, formerly a chief economic adviser at the Bank of England, who put forward the proposition that any measure of the money supply behaves differently when it becomes an official target by the very act of targeting it.

form. Attempts to regulate strictly the terms on which people may borrow from and lend to each other lead them to use other forms of assets as money. Central banks may lay down monetary targets but individuals and firms have their own ideas of the money they wish to hold. The lack of information at the disposal of the monetary authorities on the continuously changing liquidity preferences of the millions of citizens and firms in their economies means that fine-tuning of monetary policy can be as fruitless as that of fiscal policy.

And well-intentioned regulation can sometimes be destabilising. The willingness of the US monetary authorities to underwrite the deposits of their Savings and Loans institutions led to reckless and fraudulent investments. In short, central banks and developed market economies since the War have been encouraged by macro-economic theory to believe that by attempting to control what Glasner has called 'a statistical representation of a purely hypothetical construct',[14] the aggregate quantity of money, they could achieve price stability. They have found this to be largely beyond their control.

Accordingly, it appears that the monetary authorities in the UK have now abandoned macro-economic theorising, and have reverted to pragmatic and discretionary intervention, using a range of 'relevant' indicators. Despite this, monetarist theorists remain loath to accept any dilution of their earlier image of the economy 'partly because it raises questions about the adequacy of their models and the meaning of such accepted concepts as rational expectations'.[15]

Macro-economic Models

As has been pointed out many times in the past, and amply illustrated by experience, the future characteristics of a market economy – that is, an economic system made up of the decisions of millions of different human beings – are unpredictable in any precisely quantifiable sense. This simple

---

[14] D. Glasner, *Free Banking and Monetary Reform*, Cambridge: Cambridge University Press, 1989.

[15] C. Goodhart, 'The Conduct of Monetary Policy', in C.J. Green and D.T. Llewellyn (eds.), *Surveys in Monetary Economics*, Vol. One, Oxford: Blackwell, 1991.

truth did not discourage the growth in the post-war period of a miniature industry, engaged in the construction, testing, updating and operation of mathematical models of individual market economies. When fed with somehow predetermined values of their exogenous variables, these models are used to forecast values of aggregate variables for the economy concerned, usually up to a period of some two years ahead.

Such models are typically a set of simultaneous linear relationships between various aggregate variables, whose parameters are estimated by statistical 'fitting' to time-series data.

From the beginning of this activity, which may be identified with Tinbergen's experiments[16] in 1939, very large amounts of resources, both public and private, have been invested in it. In the United States in the 1960s, the Brookings Institution was reported to have a model with over 300 equations and 500 variables. It was finally laid to rest in 1972.

At the present time in the UK, some 13 different organisations produce regular forecasts based on macro-economic models.[17] The best known of those models is run by the Treasury; it comprises more than 100 individual equations, linking variables such as unemployment, inflation and the budget deficit. It is said to be tended by a team of 30 economists.

As long ago as 1957, Haberler observed of earlier macro-economic models that none stood up to the test of extrapolation beyond the period of the data from which they were constructed. Despite the immensely increased size and number of such models, together with the progress in econometric techniques claimed to have taken place since then, this conclusion remains unchanged.

Forecasting Record of Macro-Models

A recent comparative survey of the forecasting record of the major British macro-economic models by Burrell and Hall at

---

[16] J. Tinbergen, *Statistical Testing of Business Cycle Theories*, Geneva: League of Nations, 1939.

[17] Similar forecasts produced by 25 financial institutions in the City of London are also published quarterly in the *Financial Times*. It is impossible to know to what extent the latter forecasts are based on macro-economic models and to what extent on subjective judgement.

the London Business School concluded that their results could be interpreted as a

> 'damning criticism of economic forecasting. Many years of research effort do not seem to have increased confidence in relatively short-term prediction much beyond a simple trend estimation'.

Burrell and Hall go on to say:

> '[T]he record has certainly been poor; the late 1980s boom was widely under-forecast, no one anticipated the start of the recession or its depth, and the recovery was wrongly called on a number of occasions before it actually occurred.'[18]

Significantly, the forecast errors were greater than differences between the forecasts of Keynesian and monetarist modelling groups.

Other surveys come to similar conclusions. In June 1993 the OECD published the results of a survey which it had conducted of official forecasts for the growth of output and inflation one year ahead.[19] The forecasting record of the OECD itself, of the IMF, and of the governments of the seven major world economies were examined over the period 1987-92. The benchmark used for comparison was the naïve projection that next year's output growth or inflation would be the same as this year's.

In terms of output, this simple rule performed at least as well as the official forecasters. In terms of inflation, it performed as well as did the forecasts of the OECD and the IMF, and slightly better than those of the national governments.

Reviewing this record, Paul Ormerod (Director of Economics, Henley Centre for Forecasting, 1982-92) observes that

> 'the combined might of the macro-economic models and the intellectual power of their operators, whether based in national governments or installed in tax-free splendour at public expense in Paris or in the IMF in Washington, could not perform any

---

18 A. Burrell and S. Hall, 'A Comparison of Macroeconomic Forecasts', *London Business School Economic Outlook*, Vol.18, No.2, February 1994.

19 OECD, *Economic Outlook*, Vol.53, June 1993, pp.49-54.

better than the simplest possible rule which could be used to make a forecast'.[20]

Macro-economic models are particularly poor at anticipating turning points. Ormerod notes that the 1993 Japanese recession was not predicted nor was the US recovery in the second half of 1992, nor the slowdown in the first half of 1993. In Europe, models failed to predict the turmoil in the ERM, and the depth of the German recession.[21] Accordingly, the same writer is surely justified in concluding that

> 'on any normal scientific criterion, the conclusion would be drawn that conventional macro-economics, whether Keynesian or monetarist, does not offer an adequate description of the behaviour of developed economies'.[22]

Macro-Models Mislead

For many years, public opinion and governments have been misled by macro-economic models. In the light of the results achieved, it is surprising that governments should continue to be willing to fund this sort of activity with tax-payers' money. That private firms and individuals should be willing to purchase forecasts based on macro-economic models can only be attributed to an unfamiliarity with their past performance.

Is the conclusion that economic prediction is quite impossible? Generally speaking, it is not possible in economics to predict particular events – for example, particular prices or quantities at a specified future date. No economist has so far been known to have made his fortune by applying economic theory to the prediction of particular prices or quantities. Apart from the elements of chance, this is so because knowledge of the factors determining such an event is so widely disseminated. The most that can be hoped for is what Hayek has called 'pattern predictions'.[23]

There are some market traders who enjoy occasional successes, as well as less well-publicised losses, through

---

[20] P.Ormerod, *The Death of Economics*, London: Faber and Faber, 1994, p.105.

[21] Ormerod, *ibid.*, p.104.

[22] P. Ormerod, Letter to the Editor, *Financial Times*, 13 July 1993.

[23] F.A. Hayek, *Studies in Philosophy, Politics and Economics*, London: Routledge & Kegan Paul, 1967, p.261.

anticipating market movements by means of subjective judgement. It is sometimes possible for academic and other observers to discern correctly broad medium-term trends in the evolution of a particular economy. What cannot be done is to produce acceptable numerical forecasts of future events using macro-economic models. This is so for a number of reasons, notably:

o Macro-economic variables are no more than the aggregate resultant of millions of individual decisions. For this reason, relationships between such variables are not stable.

o The implicit assumption that the future behaviour of markets will be the same as in the past is not true.

o Those factors in the economic process which do not lend themselves to measurement are either omitted from the models entirely, or treated in cavalier fashion.

o In the case of econometric models, the theoretical requirements for acceptable procedures for statistical estimation of the parameters are seldom satisfied.

o The primary statistical data themselves are subject to serious inaccuracies, as evidenced by their periodic revision.

Conclusions on Policy

The achievement of full employment was the primary policy objective behind the early development of macro-economic theory. Although the major developed market economies are further from achieving this objective than they ever were in the post-war period, current discussions of policy towards unemployment no longer include macro-economic remedies.

Another tenet of macro-economic thinking was that economic growth and the business cycle are separable. We have now learned from experience that attempts to promote growth by stimulating aggregate demand lead sooner or later to inflation. It seems one cannot have the growth benefits of the market economy without accepting the cycle as an intrinsic part of the growth process.

The fine-tuning of aggregate demand through fiscal policy has long been abandoned, and the possibility of the fine-tuning of bank lending by central banks has been thrown increasingly into doubt. Indeed, in the UK it seems as if there has been an uncoupling of monetary policy from macro-economic theory.

Thus, policy-makers have discovered that macro-economics does not provide a useful framework for thinking about policy issues. While there are many different points of view on policy towards the realisation of price stability and full employment, and some of these views are held passionately, there are none which now command general support. This is perhaps because all the macro-economic policies which have been tried in Britain since the War seem to have failed. That suggests that there may be something wrong with the theories which underlie them.

IV. THE FAILURE OF
MACRO-ECONOMIC THEORY

Why Macro-economic Theory Has Failed

The reason why macro-economics has proved to be so unhelpful in thinking about questions of economic policy is that macro-economic theory is seriously defective. These defects may be divided into three broad classes.[1]

The first of these is *formalism*. One example of formalism is where a concept, such as equilibrium, devised for one context is later used inappropriately in another.[2]

The smaller the micro-economic unit the more firmly based is the concept of equilibrium. The equilibrium of the household or of the firm is a simple notion, virtually synonymous with rational action. However, to look for equilibrium in the economy as a whole is to expect too much. It may be that in some international financial markets, where arbitrage is worthwhile, equilibrating forces work strongly and swiftly. But in markets where durable and specific capital goods play a part – that is, in most of the economy – the attainment of equilibrium *even momentarily* becomes very unlikely.[3]

Another example of formalism is where abstract entities are treated as though they were real, or, conversely, where real entities are treated as though they were abstractions.

The treatment of the consumer provides an illustration of the latter. For the neo-Keynesian the consumer hardly exists at all, while for the neo-classical economist the consumer has no more than a shadowy existence. As Lachmann comments:

---

[1] This classification is due to Lachmann: L.M. Lachmann, *Macro-economic Thinking and the Market Economy*, Hobart Paper No.56, London: Institute of Economic Affairs, 1973.

[2] *c.f.* Marshall's observation, quoted by Edgeworth, on the use of mathematics in economics: 'When the actual conditions of particular problems have not been studied, such (mathematical) knowledge is little better than a derrick for sinking oil wells where there are no oil-bearing strata'. (Reprinted in J.Eastwell, M.Milgate and P.Newman (eds.), *The New Palgrave, A Dictionary of Economics*, Vol.3, London: Macmillan, 1987, p.405.)

[3] Lachmann, *op.cit.*, p.16.

'Once his preference scales have been fully recorded, he is dismissed into the realms of shadows, and told never to come back. It is characteristic of the formalistic style of thought that those who have imbibed it have become incapable of conceiving of spontaneous human action, as distinct from reaction to outside events.'[4]

The second major defect of macro-economic theory is the *method of abstraction*. While the permissible level of abstraction depends on the problem at hand, two normal rules of procedure are both violated by macro-economic thinking. The first concerns the degree of abstraction: from an initial level of abstraction it must be possible gradually to approach reality by modifying one's initial assumptions. The second concerns what is being left out: one may not abstract from essentials. The baby must not be thrown out along with the bath water. Amongst the important economic variables habitually left out by macro-economics are entrepreneurship, institutions and most psychological factors, together with that essential characteristic of the developed market economy, the incessant introduction of new goods and new processes.

Thirdly, there is the implicit *assumption* that the aggregates in which macro-theory deals are *of unchanging composition*. Both neo-Keynesians and neo-classicals regard as 'macro-variables' what are in reality the cumulative results of millions of individual actions. Since these micro-economic actions do not repeat themselves on a daily or monthly basis, and certainly not annually, these is no reason to believe in the aggregate constancy of the macro-variables over time. The changing composition of aggregates such as gross domestic product (GDP) or gross investment affects the values of other variables in the economy as much or more than do changes in the aggregates themselves. So far as GDP is concerned, it is quite normal in a developed economy to find declining industries side by side with rapidly expanding ones.

Schumpeter pointed out the limitations of assuming that all the effects on economic activity as a whole that emanate from the multitude of individual investment decisions (positive and negative) can be measured by their algebraic sum.[5] Say, for

---

[4] Lachmann, *op. cit.*, p.22.

[5] J.A. Schumpeter, *History of Economic Analysis*, New York: Oxford University Press, 1954, p.279.

example, that aggregate investment amounted to zero. The effects would be very different if this result was produced by all firms investing zero, or if some firms invested positively while others dis-invested. Furthermore, the effects would be different again to the extent that the investments were predominantly complementary to, or competing with, existing capacity.

There are two other important variables, expectations and profits, where the assumption of constant composition is particularly misleading. In fact, expectations differ between individuals and change over time:

> 'In a market economy there is a central market for shares in capital combinations, the stock exchange, in which the prices of these shares, governed by a balance of expectations between "bulls" and "bears", is fixed anew every day. As this balance of expectation tilts from day to day, so do prices.'[6]

Since their basis is to be found primarily in the ever-changing pattern of price-cost differences in thousands of different markets, profits are pre-eminently a micro-economic phenomenon which can have no place in a long-term equilibrium world. A macro-economic theory of profit can make little sense and an equilibrium rate of profit is a contradiction in terms. Contrary to the assumptions of an aggregate production function, there is no such thing as '*the*' rate of profit, only *rates* of profit, which can and do differ widely from each other because of the heterogeneity of the capital stock.

These defects of macro-economic theory are not new. Before Lachmann, they have been pointed out at various times by Mises,[7] Hayek,[8] and Schumpeter,[9] amongst others. Yet, as

---

6 Lachmann, *op.cit.*, pp.52-53.

7 L. von Mises (1912), *Theory of Money and Credit*, New Haven, CT: Yale University Press, 1953.

8 '[Macro-economics] gives us a useful approximation to the facts, but as a theoretical explanation of causal connections [it] is unsatisfactory and sometimes misleading, because it asserts empirically observed correlations with no justification for the belief that they will always occur.' (F.A.Hayek, *The Denationalisation of Money*, London: Institute of Economic Affairs, Hobart Paper No.70, 3rd edn., 1990, p.80 (n.3).)

9 Schumpeter (1954), *op. cit.*, p.280.

we shall see in the following section, after the Keynesian version of macro-economic theory had been largely discredited, the development of macro-economic theory not only failed to address these defects, but actually aggravated them. The introduction of the rational expectations hypothesis heightened the degree of abstraction, while the extension of equilibrium concepts to the explanation of such phenomena as the failure of labour markets to clear represents a further step in the direction of formalism. Even Solow, one of those who laid the foundations of modern macro-economics, has expressed his disquiet.[10]

The 'New' Macro-economics

Between the late 1960s and the late 1980s macro-economic theorising became both broader and deeper. The main objective of the 'new' macro-economics, as it came to be known, was to establish micro-economic foundations for the subject. Its two principal features were the introduction of rational expectations, and an attempt to explain macro-economic phenomena within the context of equilibrium models where wages and prices adjust instantaneously to equate supply and demand.

Reviewing these developments in 1988, in two separate but contemporaneous review articles, Mankiw[11] and Fischer[12] both claimed that remarkable progress had been made in understanding many theoretical issues, but were candid enough to admit that in understanding the actual causes of macro-economic fluctuations and in applying macro-economics to policy-making '...there is greater not less confusion'.[13]

Fischer attributes this disappointing conclusion to two factors. One is 'the increasing realisation of the extraordinary difficulty of settling disputes with econometric evidence'. Amongst the remedies he suggests, the 'obvious possibilities' include 'careful case studies of particular episodes'.

---

[10] R.M. Solow, *Growth Theory*, Oxford: Oxford University Press, 1988, p. xvi.

[11] N.G. Mankiw, 'Recent Developments in Macro-economics', *Journal of Money, Credit and Banking*, Vol.20, No.3, August 1988.

[12] S. Fischer, 'Recent Developments in Macro-economics', *Economic Journal*, Vol.98, June 1988, pp.294-339.

[13] Fischer, *ibid.*, p.331.

Second, he complains that it has become fashionable to say that economists have little to offer on the policy issues of the day. But macro-economists cannot leave policy issues to those who are 'ignorant or unscrupulous enough to claim full understanding of the issues', and 'macro-economists will not be able to participate seriously in such analyses without the use of models, small or large, that attempt to quantify the impact of policy decisions'.[14]

Two observations are in order here. First, practitioners of macro-economic policy are only too well aware of the uncertainty which surrounds the taking of macro-policy decisions. To judge by their pronouncements, it is macro-economic *theorists* who are much more confident that they fully understand the issues. Second, the claim that macro-economic models are needed to quantify the impact of policy decisions begs the question of whether these models give results which are useful, or even adequate. As we have seen, the evidence suggests that they do not.

Both Mankiw and Fischer recognise that the developments in macro-economic theory in the last 25 years will be judged by the extent to which they prove useful to applied macro-economists. As explained in Section III, this has not been the case. What about the claim that the 'new' macro-economics represents theoretical progress over the old?

We must first ask to what extent the search for micro-foundations has been successful. Fischer states:

'...the earlier notion that once the microeconomic foundations had been laid, a set of standard macro-models could be used, has not been justified. Rather the tendency has been to build a variety of micro-based models each making or emphasising a specific point'.[15]

In fact, the search for a Walrasian micro-foundation has ended in a theoretical cul-de-sac. Although the literature of the new macro-economics is replete with such phrases as '*the* equilibrium' and '*the* natural rate' and with discussions as to how long the economy will take to return to '*the* equilibrium', the implicit assumptions of the uniqueness and stability of such an equilibrium have no theoretical justification, as

---

[14] Fischer, *ibid.*, p.331.

[15] Fischer, *ibid.*, p.330.

Kirman points out.[16] In failing to overcome this aggregation problem, the neo-classical equilibrium theorists therefore seem to have painted themselves into a corner, the instrument of their so doing being the straitjacket of classical mechanics.

The use of equilibrium models to explain macro-economic phenomena is one of the major developments within the new macro-economics identified by Mankiw. To those not constrained by this line of thinking, the method of equilibrium seems particularly unsuited to the investigation of phenomena concerning the lack of co-ordination of economic activity. The attempt to model what are clearly disequilibrium phenomena by equilibrium methods has not surprisingly led to some absurd implications, such as that the unemployed may be voluntarily increasing their leisure time.

The Rational Expectations Axiom

The other major development has been the widespread adoption of the axiom of rational expectations.[17] The Rational Expectations hypothesis epitomises much of what is wrong with macro-economic thinking. It does not pretend to offer an independent view of how agents actually form their expectations. Instead, it is a device for making the process of expectation formation consistent with the existing (neo-classical) theory.

In order to do this, it is obliged to assert that all agents possess the same knowledge of the 'true' model of how the economy works. As evidence to the contrary, the *Financial Times* publishes quarterly the results of some 40 different macro-economic models[18] of how the British economy works (see Section III, subsection entitled 'Macro-economic Models', above, p. 27).

---

[16] A. Kirman, 'The Intrinsic Limits of Modern Economic Theory', *Economic Journal*, Vol.99, No.395, 1989.

[17] This proposition asserts that individuals, when making decisions, possess all the relevant information that they require, including knowledge of the structure of the economic system. Any errors in their analysis of that information are attributable to random influences.

[18] These models are linear. Should the 'correct' model of the economy prove to be non-linear, the possibility of accurate prediction almost vanishes: see D.Parker & R.Stacey, *Chaos, Management and Economics*, Hobart Paper No.125, London: Institute of Economic Affairs, 1994, p.49.

The rational expectations hypothesis assumes that agents acquire their 'correct' knowledge of how the market truly works through the experience of market participation. The implicit assumption is that markets exhibit repetitive behaviour. While this might be a plausible assumption in a primitive subsistence economy, it can hardly be sustained in an evolving market economy. And differences in observed behaviour between competing firms in the same industry must presumably be attributable to differences between each company's perception of its business environment.

In view of these limitations, it is not surprising that Phelps[19] should have described the rational expectations movement as a religion rather than a scientific enterprise. The conclusion must therefore be that the theoretical progress claimed by the proponents of the new macro-economics is no more than an incomplete journey towards methodological unity rather than any progress towards providing a theoretical framework useful for the understanding of actual phenomena. This conclusion is borne out by the history of developments in macro-economic monetary theory and macro-economic growth theory.

Monetary Theory

The lack of success which has attended the efforts of monetary authorities everywhere as they have sought to control the aggregate supply of money (see Section III, subsection entitled 'Unemployment Unexplained', above, p.21) can be attributed directly to the hold exercised over their minds by the quantity theory of money, a macro-economic theory which long antedates the Keynesian revolution.

The quantity theory rose to prominence in the middle of the 19th century in opposition to the then prevailing classical theory.[20] Implicit in the theory was an unfavourable view of the rôle of competition in the supply of money. In this view, controlling the quantity of money should be the operational objective of government policy, and under the Bank Charter Act of 1844 the Bank of England was given monopoly power

---

[19] E. Phelps, 'Comment' in *Journal of Money, Credit and Banking*, Vol.20, No.3, August 1988.

[20] Much of this section draws upon D. Glasner's *Free Banking and Monetary Reform, op. cit.*

over the issue of notes. It did not regulate bank deposits, which continued to expand in response to market forces. The quantity theory thus had little practical effect until after the Great Depression, an experience which provided the political impetus for suppressing competition in the supply of bank deposits.

An important element in Keynes's *General Theory* was the explicit assumption that the nominal quantity of money was a policy instrument under the complete control of the monetary authority. However, once they had gained absolute control over their monetary systems after the Second World War, governments exploited that control to generate increasing inflation. High inflation, which raised the cost of holding government-supplied or government-regulated deposits, then unleashed a competitive response that has overcome the regulatory barriers erected to suppress competition in the supply of money.[21]

When the Keynesian orthodoxy was later challenged by the monetarist counter-revolution in the 1970s, the consensus between them that the monetary system and the nominal quantity of money had to be kept under the strict control of government was reinforced, despite the otherwise well-publicised differences between the two schools of thought.

The common assumption shared by macro-economists, whether monetarist or Keynesian, is that

(1) there is a uniquely identifiable quantity of money; and

(2) the monetary authority has full control over this quantity.[22]

I will examine these assumptions in turn.

---

[21] Glasner, *ibid*, p.xi.

[22] While some macro-economists, notably the late Karl Brunner, have attempted to integrate institutional arrangements into their analysis of the money supply process, and while some textbooks (but not all) recognise that the money supply is determined not only by central bank policy but also by the behaviour of individuals who hold money and of the banks in which money is held, in the academic literature full central bank control is the normal assumption. For example, Blanchard and Fischer write: 'in all cases we assume that the central bank controls the quantity of money'. (O.Blanchard and S.Fischer, *Lectures on Macroeconomics*, Cambridge: MIT Press, 1989, p.570.)

In a lengthy chapter reviewing definitions of money, Friedman and Schwartz[23] reject any *a priori* approach; they argue that what is defined as money is just a matter of analytical convenience. In their own earlier analysis, their choice was based on practical grounds: 'the availability of comparable data for a long period.'[24] They nowhere address the long-standing criticism of the concept of money as an aggregate quantity. What Machlup[25] has called the quality of 'moneyness' pertains to different financial assets in different degrees; it is wrong to think that the various media of exchange can be added up into one single sum. We have already seen (Section III, subsection entitled 'Developments in Monetary Policy', above, p. 25) into what difficulties monetary authorities have fallen when they have attempted to identify money with a particular class of asset.

There is an implicit presumption in the monetarist version of macro-economic thinking that the authorities can impose on a market economy any interest rate they wish. This presumption presumably follows from the habit of thinking that there is only one interest rate, which in the IS/LM model simultaneously clears the money, bond and (with a horizontal aggregate supply curve) output markets.

In fact, there exists an array of market-clearing interest rates, and the monetary authorities exert a direct influence over only a sub-set of these – the rates at which they supply marginal funds to the banking system. Accordingly, the market interest rates which impinge upon real activity are distinct from, though not independent of, this administered rate.

Thus, market rates are not directly controlled by the monetary authorities, but are determined in part by

---

[23] M. Friedman and A. Schwartz, *Monetary Statistics of the United States*, New York: Columbia University Press, 1970.

[24] M. Friedman and A. Schwartz, *A Monetary History of the United States 1867-1960*, Princeton: Princeton University Press, 1963, p.151.

[25] F. Machlup, 'Euro-Dollar Creation, A Mystery Story', *Banca Nazionale del Lavoro Quarterly Review*, No.94, 1970. Recent experiments in forming weighted aggregates of different classes of monetary assets have gone some way towards meeting this criticism. However, these have not so far been shown to be any better at predicting inflation than the conventional monetary aggregates. (See P. Fisher, S. Hudson and M. Pradhan, 'Divisia Indices for Money: An Appraisal of Theory and Practice', *Working Paper Series* No.9, London: Bank of England, 1993.) (See also Section V, subsection entitled 'Money', below, p. 57.)

behavioural relations between individual agents in the private sector. Consequently, without knowing the relationships between the official interest rates set by the authorities and the market rates impinging on the real economy, it is difficult to judge the appropriate movement in official rates necessary to achieve a given impact on the real economy.

The relationships between the commercial banks and the rest of the private sector are a vital element in the transmission mechanism of changes in the quantity of money through to changes in prices or outputs: it is likely that these relationships will vary across sectors, over the cycle and through time.[26]

A middle-of-the-road consensus amongst macro-economists has formed round the view that while in the long run the impact of monetary changes will be absorbed in prices, in the medium term monetary policy can have an effect on the level and direction of economic activity. For example, an expansionary monetary policy, by lowering rates of return on bonds and raising the prices of equities, will encourage investment, thus raising the level of real output.

Insofar as this argument is conducted within the framework outlined above, it has hardly advanced beyond the original statement of the proposition by David Hume.[27] In fact, as Tobin has shown,[28] the possible impacts of monetary changes on economic activity are varied and complex, because they depend on the exact response of the whole structure of rates of return on competing assets to the monetary change, and to the possible reactions of these changes in rates of return on decisions to consume and invest.

Macro-Theory of Money – Further Limitations

The macro-economic theory of money has further limitations. *First*, there is the need to disaggregate. In order to know the extent to which an increase in the money supply may be inflationary or may lead to an increase in output, it is also necessary to know how it will be spent. For example, is it devoted to an increase in productive capacity – in which case

---

[26] S. Dale and A.G. Haldane, 'Interest Rate Control in a Model of Monetary Policy', *Working Paper Series* No.17, Bank of England, 1993, p.28.

[27] D. Hume, 'Of Money', in E. Rotwein (ed.), *Writings on Economics*, London, Nelson, 1955.

[28] J. Tobin, *Essays in Economics*, Vol. One, Amsterdam: North Holland, 1971.

the resultant output coming on to the market will have a disinflationary effect, or is it devoted to an increase in consumption, in which case the inflationary effect can be expected to be permanent?

Second, the macro-economic version of the quantity theory distracts attention from the need to analyse the transmission mechanism through which an increase in the quantity of money influences the *relative* demand for different goods and services, and hence the set of relative prices as well as the aggregate price level. By considering only the effects of changes in the quantity of money on the *aggregate* price level, attention is diverted from the misdirection of resources caused by inflation, and thus from the origins of the unemployment which eventually results, as inflation subsides.

Third, channels of influence run in both directions, not only from money to economic activity but also from economic activity to money. A satisfactory theory of money should, therefore, achieve a synthesis of this mutual interaction. Yet macro-economic theorists generally prefer to consider only a single direction of causality, from money to economic activity.[29]

If the primary objective of monetary policy is price stability – that is, keeping constant an aggregate index of prices – as currently seems to be the case throughout most of the Western

---

[29] Friedman and Schwartz (1963), *op.cit*, p.695, recognise that 'while the influence running from money to economic activity has been predominant, there have clearly also been influences running the other way ...', but writing about the crucial period 1929-33, they conclude, 'there is one sense – and, so far as we can see, only one – in which a case can be made for the proposition that the monetary decline was a consequence of the economic decline. That sense is not relevant to our main task of seeking to understand economic relations, since it involves relying primarily on psychological and political factors' (p.69). Later in the same volume, Hellinger comments: 'I am a businessman ... my background compels me to place much greater weight upon these "psychological and political factors" than the authors would be willing to concede ... It has been burned in upon me that monetary policy, in final analysis, acts on man whose conduct is not predictable; it neither operates in a vacuum nor in a world in which all other factors can be taken as constant' (Friedman and Schwartz, *op.cit.*, p.809). Hellinger also quotes approvingly a passage from a British Government report attributable to D.H. Robertson: '... economic restraints and incentives operate on men's' minds where it is not possible to forecast their precise effects: they operate also in circumstances which are constantly changing.' (*Third Report of the Council on Prices, Productivity and Incomes*, London: HMSO, July 1959, p.25, para.73.)

world, then it is wrong to believe that this would be achieved by maintaining a constant, or constantly changing, stock of money, even if that could somehow be identified (which it cannot). To achieve the desired result in terms of an index of prices, the quantity of money would have to be kept such that people would not have to reduce or increase their outlays (in aggregate) for the purpose of adapting their cash balances to their (continuously changing) liquidity preferences.[30] No single body, such as a monetary authority, could possibly have in advance all the information necessary continuously to adjust the supply of money to bring about such a result. Only a market can discover what the necessary amount of money should be.

Growth Theory

As well as taking over that part of economics concerned with business cycles, macro-economics in the early post-war period proceeded to colonise another important area of the subject, namely, the theory of economic growth. In this branch of economics, the methodological limitations of macro-economic theory should have been particularly obvious, but the seductive simplicity of a few algebraic relationships appears to have blinded many economists to these considerations.

Steady State Growth

It was the Swedish economist Gustav Cassell[31] who, in 1912, first put forward the notion of a steadily growing economy, as a logical extension of the concept of the stationary state. The idea in steady state growth is that output in each sector of the economy grows at the same constant rate as does the stock of capital, the supply of labour and all other aggregate inputs, so that the whole system exhibits a moving equilibrium through time. This idea was rediscovered by Harrod[32] in 1939, and formed the basis of a subsequent torrent of books and articles from the late 1950s to the 1970s, ostensibly on the subject of economic growth, but in practice all sharing the characteristic limitations of the steady state growth model.

---

[30] F.A. Hayek (1990), *op. cit.*, p.81.

[31] G. Cassell, *The Theory of Social Economy*, London: T. F. Unwin, 1923, Ch.I.

[32] R.F. Harrod, 'An Essay In Dynamic Theory', *Economic Journal*, March 1939.

Significantly, Abramowitz omitted steady state models from his 1952 survey of the theory of economic growth for the American Economic Association, recognising that *'they offer no explanation or prediction of the way in which actual economies have developed or are likely to develop over time'*.[33]

Thirteen years later, when Hahn and Matthews came to the same task of surveying growth theory, they confined themselves exclusively to a survey of steady state models. In so doing, they recognised that the literature they were surveying was different from that 'which would be used if the immediate purpose was to provide the best available explanation of the variety of historical growth experience', adding rather lamely that 'the authors of these models have naturally had in mind as a rule that their work should contribute to an understanding of the way economies actually grow over time'.[34]

By the end of the 1970s the torrent of publications on steady state theory had slowed to a trickle, and one of the principal exponents of the theory, Robert Solow, noted in 1982 that 'there were definite signs that it was just about played out'.[35] In his review of this literature in his 1987 Nobel Prize address, Solow appeared to question the usefulness of some of the fundamental characteristics of balanced growth theory, namely, equilibrium growth paths and steady states. He also acknowledged the limitations of econometric analyses of historical time-series data and the need to augment them with 'direct observation of the way economic institutions work'.[36]

Neither of these concerns was addressed by the second wave of steady state growth models. While in the early neo-classical models the long-run rate of growth of output per head was determined outside the model by the rate of accumulation of knowledge, the 'new' growth theory sought to determine the rate of technical progress within the model. Whereas it was an inference of the 'old' growth theory that all countries with access to the same technology should have converging

[33] M. Abramowitz, 'The Theory of Economic Growth', in H.S. Ellis (ed.), *A Survey of Contemporary Economics*, Homewood, Ill.: Irwin, 1952.

[34] F. Hahn and R.C.O. Matthews, *The Theory of Economic Growth, A Survey*, in *AEA Surveys of Economic Theory*, Vol.2, New York: Macmillan, 1965.

[35] R.M. Solow, 'Growth Theory', in D. Greenaway and I. Stewart (eds.), *Companion to Contemporary Economic Thought*, London: Routledge, 1991.

[36] R.M. Solow (1988), *op. cit.*, p.xvi.

productivity growth rates, the new growth theories permitted divergences in growth rates between countries of different sizes. But they did so by introducing specific and often arbitrary assumptions, chosen for their convenience in order to bring about the desired conclusion.[37]

For example, an essential feature of Romer's 1986 model[38] is that the intangible asset, knowledge, exhibits increasing marginal productivity. In order to prevent this assumption from producing implausible consequences, the author is obliged to impose a number of restrictions including the requirement that the growth potential generated cannot be too large relative to the discount rate.

Again, Aghion and Howitt make the special assumption that when an innovation occurs it allows a uniform cost reduction in all intermediate goods in a given time-period.[39] These innovations occur randomly in time. Unfortunately, one of the results of this model is that the average growth rate increases with the size of the economy. Solow is moved to observe that 'the world does not seem to work like that'.[40]

From all this literature no-one has been able to point to a single contribution which has been made to an improved understanding of the way economies have *actually* grown over time.

This is scarcely surprising since steady state growth theory, the only type of growth theory recognised by macro-economics, excludes not just some, but *all* of the essential features which characterise growth in a market economy.

Market Economy Growth: Qualitative Change

The first essential feature of growth in a market economy is qualitative change in most of the principal variables in the economic system. New goods and new technologies and new

---

[37] 'There is no reason to assume they are descriptively valid, or that their implications have significant robustness against equally plausible variations in assumptions'. (Solow (1991), *op.cit*, p.412.)

[38] P. Romer, 'Increasing Returns and Long Run Growth', *Journal of Political Economy*, Vol.94, 1986, pp.1,002-37.

[39] P. Aghion and P. Howitt,'A Model of Growth Through Creative Destruction', *Econometrica*, Vol.60, No.2, March 1992.

[40] Solow (1991), *op.cit.*, p.411.

methods of distribution are constantly replacing existing ones; new markets are opened and new sources of supply of primary resources are exploited. Qualitative change cannot adequately be represented by some corresponding quantitative change. No matter how many valves are added to a radio, they do not equal a silicon chip.

Second, growth is characterised by uncertainty. In the typical balanced growth model, there is perfect foresight, but in a world of change the future is unknowable. Changes in demand, in technology, in resource availability, in new goods and services and in new processes of production cannot be predicted. In the absence of certainty, people form expectations about the future, and different people form different expectations. The expectations of some investors will prove to be correct and they will make capital gains. Others will be disappointed, and they will make losses. This is not consistent with the continuous equilibrium in every time-period which is the key feature of steady state models.

The third essential feature of the market economy is that because growth means change, it is disruptive and subversive of existing patterns of behaviour, and is marked by discontinuities.

The fourth essential feature is that the process of growth is both influenced by the institutions and attitudes of the society in which it takes place, and at the same time alters them. There is thus a cumulative process of interaction between economic, institutional and psychological factors. Amongst the more important elements in this process are entrepreunership and profit-seeking activity.

The history of the developed market economy in every country is a history of booms and slumps, as well as of continuing shifts in sectoral sizes, as exemplified by the decline of agriculture and the growth of the public sector. And one of the best-established of all empirical propositions in economics is that consumption proportions change as income increases over time.

Since all of these characteristic features of economic growth are omitted from steady state growth models, it is not surprising that they should fail to represent even the most superficial characteristics of actual growth as it takes place in market economies.

In a recent review of the 'new' growth theory, Solow concedes that it falls short of a model ready for econometric testing with historical time-series. But he claims for it another 'respectable' rôle, as a 'guide to intuition and ... therefore to observation and interpretation'.[41]

But the new growth theory has no original insights of its own to contribute. All it does is try to squeeze the intuition of earlier 'literary' economists into a mathematical straitjacket. In so doing, it is forced to exclude all but a few elements of these insights, and drastically to oversimplify the relationships. For example, Aghion and Howitt's attempt[42] to model Schumpeter's vision of creative destruction can only be described as a caricature, whilst Romer's modelling of the myriad subtle processes of the invention and dissemination of new knowledge[43] does not add to but subtracts from our understanding of those processes.[44]

Conclusions on Growth

All the defects of macro-economic theory are exhibited to the full in growth theory. Reading the steady state growth theory whose assumptions and methods remove it so far from the characteristic patterns of growth observed in market economies, one wonders what is the point of this type of formalisation? Solow maintains that 'without formalisation, there is no way of identifying the implications of these ideas sufficiently precisely to evaluate them'.[45] But such precision may be attained at the price of truth. And we have seen that such growth models have failed to produce hypotheses which can be tested by methods their proponents would approve. Recent developments of the theory have only exacerbated these defects. The resulting closer adherence which is claimed to the stylised aggregate facts is achieved at the cost of introducing arbitrary special restrictions.

---

[41] Solow (1991), *op.cit.*, p.412.

[42] Aghion and Howitt, *op.cit.*, p.349. See also Section V, subsection entitled 'Growth and Cycle', below, p. 53.

[43] P. Romer, *op. cit.*, pp. 1,014-16.

[44] Compare, for example, the work of Rosenberg on this subject, such as in N. Rosenberg, *Exploring the Black Box*, Cambridge University Press, 1994.

[45] Solow (1991), *op.cit.*, p.406.

The new growth theory only represents 'progress' over the 'old' for those who believe that progress in economics is represented by the application of the methods of the natural sciences. As Hayek pointed out more than half a century ago, that is a fundamental misconception.[46]

The process of increasing refinement which has characterised macro-economics as well as micro-economics since the War, has meant a process by which a growing number of influential factors are excluded from the analysis, and increasingly artificial and implausible assumptions are introduced into it. In the case of steady state growth theory, insistence upon rigid adherence to equilibrium paths has precluded consideration of short-run departures from equilibrium, whilst the exclusion of institutional variables such as entrepreneurship has disqualified it from offering a convincing explanation of long-run economic growth.

Conclusions

Critics have long pointed to the fundamental defects of macro-economic theory, namely, undue formalism, a tendency to abstract from essentials, the assumption of the unchanging composition of aggregates, and the neglect of any micro-economic foundations. While it was the desire to provide micro-economic foundations which drove the development of macro-economic theory in the 1970s and 1980s, we have seen that this was an attempt which has failed.

Macro-economic theory has not attempted to address its other, more serious, defects. In the mistaken belief that it should mimic the methods of the natural sciences, especially physics, it has abstracted from essential but non-quantifiable variables, and treated a sequence of historical events as if it was repetitive, deterministic and reversible.

Macro-economic theory has gone down a *cul-de-sac* of increasing formalism and heightened levels of abstraction. It has thereby moved further away from the possibility of offering a satisfactory explanation of activity in the real economy. Macro-economics is one of those approaches which, in Lachmann's words '...are inadequate to their subject matter

---

[46] F.A. Hayek, 'Scientism and the Study of Society', part I, *Economica*, Vol.9, 1942, pp.267-91; part II, *Economica*, Vol.10, 1943, pp.34-63; part III, *Economica*, Vol.11, 1944, pp.27-39.

since their conceptual tools do not permit those who handle them to grapple with important features of the subject'.[47]

The consequences of these developments have been to obscure rather than to clarify thinking about the economy, to separate theory from policy, and to cause policy-makers to look elsewhere for enlightenment. It has also caused increasing dissatisfaction amongst students of economics. The most serious effect of the predominance of macro-economic thinking has been that it has crowded out alternative modes of thought, thereby preventing a better understanding of our economic problems. The time has now come for the development of a new framework of analysis.

---

[47] Lachmann, *op.cit.*, p.51.

V. THE CLASSICAL ALTERNATIVE

The Basic Principles

An economy is composed of individual human beings who are members of households and firms (as workers, managers, entrepreneurs, and suppliers of capital) which interact through markets. They also operate in the political process through interest groups to form institutions of government.[1]

These human agents and institutions interact with an external environment which includes the framework of legal and political institutions, the developing body of scientific and technical knowledge (nowadays evolving very rapidly), the physical environment (evolving very slowly), and the rest of the world. Thus, we can think of households, firms and government as primary economic agents carrying out their activities within the framework of a set of evolving economic institutions.

The human agents at the centre of this system cannot anticipate how the interaction of these evolving institutions at all levels will turn out. Thus all human agents operate in a context of uncertainty which, beyond certain limits, is irreducible. With the rate of change of institutions and technology accelerating in the modern age, the degree of uncertainty may be considered to be increasing over time in most contemporary market economies.

It is precisely this uncertainty which gives an entrepreneurial element to every human action. In neo-classical economics, whose method is derived from classical mechanics and whose substance has been described as a cross between utilitarianism and the differential calculus, the individual chooses to 'act rationally' only in the sense that an appropriately programmed computer can 'choose' the optimal route through which to travel to its given destination. It does this with the aid of complete certainty or perfect information.

In the uncertain world in which all economic activity occurs, people do not 'choose' in this neo-classical sense,

---

[1] R.A. Gordon, 'Rigor and Relevance in a Changing Institutional Setting', *American Economic Review*, Vol. 66, No.1, March 1976.

rather they 'act'. It is this entrepreneurial element in every human action – 'the element which transforms mechanical decisions into human actions' – which

> 'maintains the subjectivist freedom of the individual decision and yet explains the emergence of those powerful regularities which economic science has, for 200 years and more, made it its business to explain'.[2]

The driving forces producing the continuing changes which characterise the process of economic growth in market economies are several, but are primarily human motivations (notably self-interest), the desire for action, and the desire of the individual to better him or herself, and to improve the material conditions of life.

These human motivations operate within, and react to, a particular situation – that is, an 'environment' in the widest sense of all the categories mentioned above. In so reacting, a qualitative change in the immediate environment may be brought about, thus creating a new situation within which the same psychological forces will continue to operate. Thus the development of the economic system and its surrounding environment may be seen as an evolutionary process in which institutions are primarily what evolve.

This was broadly the view of most economists down to and including Adam Smith, followed by Menger and later Schumpeter and Hayek. In view of the current fashion for 'institutional' or 'evolutionary' economics, it may be wondered why one of these adjectives is not used to characterise the present approach. The answer is that to use either could suggest too narrow or too broad an approach.[3] I prefer the term 'Classical' partly because I have used it before[4] but mainly because I believe this appropriately represents the tradition epitomised by Adam Smith, in which economic growth is the central subject of study, it is recognised to be an historical process, and the evolution of institutions plays a

---

[2] I.M. Kirzner, 'Subjectivism, Freedom, and Economic Law', *The South African Journal of Economics*, Vol. 60, No.1, 1992.

[3] For example, G.M. Hodgson, *Economics and Evolution*, Cambridge: Polity Press, 1993, emphasises biology as a model for studying the evolution of institutions, whereas history may provide a better example.

[4] D. Simpson, *The Political Economy of Growth*, Oxford: Blackwell, 1983.

central rôle in the process. This is a perspective shared by all of the aforementioned economists. The later classical school, notably Ricardo and Mill, lost interest in the question of economic growth and made the theory of value, later excessively refined by the neo-classical school, the centre of attention.

Growth and Cycle

In the market economy, as Schumpeter[5] reminds us, fluctuations are inseparable from growth. Any attempt, therefore, to separate trend and cycle diminishes our understanding of the process.

It is a mistake to look for general causes of booms and recessions; these are nearly always quite particular. At one time it may be an act of government, such as the deregulation of Europe's banks in the early 1980s, at another time it may be brought about by property speculation, or yet again an external shock such as a sharp increase in the price of a primary commodity. Each time the causes may be different.

What is general is the mechanism according to which both growth and instability take place. While it is true enough, as macro-economists maintain, that some growth in aggregate output takes place as a result of the annual addition to the aggregate capital stock and aggregate supply of labour in every economy, this phenomenon is overshadowed because growth consists pre-eminently of the re-organisation of production through innovation.

Innovation means qualitative change in the principal elements of the growth process; it is a phenomenon entirely ignored in macro-economics. It can take many forms.[6] One is the introduction of a new good, or of an improvement in the quality of an existing good. Another is the introduction of a new process of production or of distribution. Another is the opening up of a new market to a hitherto excluded source of supply.

Yet another is the exploitation of a new source of raw materials, such as a new oil field coming on stream. There is also the reorganisation of an industry through the formation

---

5 J.A. Schumpeter, *The Theory of Economic Development*, London: Oxford University Press, 1934.

6 Schumpeter, *ibid.*, Ch.2.

[53]

of mergers and alliances amongst some of the companies which compose it – that is, institutional innovation.

What all forms of innovation have in common is that they occur at the expense of existing activities. Not only does the new activity bid resources away from existing activities, but more importantly the output of the new activity competes on the market with the output of existing activities.

The 'Disruption' of Innovation

Competition through innovation is therefore disruptive. New products appearing on the market displace existing products in sales to consumers, while new processes undercut the costs of existing ones. In both cases, firms undertaking the new activities prosper at the expense of rival firms following older activities, the latter being forced to reduce their output and lay off workers. The least efficient of the old firms will go out of business altogether, thus rendering their specific capital worthless. This competitive process, aptly described as 'creative destruction',[7] not only represents the essential features of how growth takes place in every market economy, but at the same time explains in large part its fluctuations.

If innovations took place in a steady stream through time, then output in the market economy might be less likely to exhibit a pattern of irregular cycles. But innovations tend to occur in clusters. Partly this is because objective opportunities do occur irregularly, since breakthroughs in the discovery (or more often in the application) of the underlying technology or political events, such as the establishment of the Single European Market, do not occur evenly through time. Partly it is because entrepreneurs tend to perceive these opportunities at one and the same time. There is also at work a herd instinct amongst entrepreneurs, and indeed amongst market participants generally. If one or two head off in one direction, the rest follow. This type of behaviour is manifested very clearly in financial markets.

It is this clustering of entrepreneurial activity which is mainly responsible for the cyclical pattern of prosperity and recession which is characteristic of the developed market

---

[7] J.A. Schumpeter, *Capitalism, Socialism and Democracy*, London: Allen & Unwin, 1976, Ch.7.

[54]

economy. The entrepreneurs who are the early innovators in any new venture soon attract a host of imitators. The expenditure incurred by innovators and imitators alike in order to bid resources away from their existing uses adds to the money supply and sets in motion a boom which has both inflationary and real elements. As the boom develops, reinforced by speculative activity, some new ventures will be undertaken which will prove to be sustainable only so long as the inflation lasts. Once the banks start to get cold feet about continuing to extend credit or the authorities clamp down, the down-swing of the cycle will be aggravated by the deflationary effects of the new competing output coming onto the market and competing with existing sources of supply.

In the succeeding recession, some of the new activities will be revealed to be viable, while others will not. It is in this sense that one can speak of a 'remedial' recession following on from a boom.

This still leaves the problem of the redundant resources which had been drawn into non-viable activities, or which had previously been engaged in older activities, now rendered non-viable by the innovations. Those resources that are specific lose all their value, those that are transferable may still have a value, but the transfer costs may not be negligible.

The nature, timing and extent of the fluctuations will depend intimately upon the prevailing institutional arrangements, and the motives, expectations and values held by the human agents affected by these processes. The consequences of a disturbance of a given nature and magnitude would be very different in the contemporary 'mixed' economy of the advanced countries than they would be in the circumstances of the 'purer' capitalism of a century ago.

Even within so short a space of time as five years, the institutions and attitudes characteristic of any given contemporary economy can alter sufficiently to affect significantly the consequences of any specific act of monetary or fiscal policy. The consequences of a given change in the rate of interest will be quite different in an environment where, for example, the influence of trade unions has greatly diminished, or where attitudes to work have changed; it may be different again five years hence. What these different consequences may be can be understood only by an analysis which explicitly takes such factors into account.

[55]

One must also mention the rôle of governments in creating, or exacerbating, fluctuations in economic activity. It now seems widely agreed that mismanagement of monetary policy by the federal authorities made the Great Depression in the United States more severe than it might otherwise have been. Today, attempts at fine-tuning of monetary and fiscal policies can sometimes be destabilising. In the UK, voters have become accustomed to a 'political business cycle' since the Second World War. Governments seeking re-election use monetary or fiscal policies to give a short-term stimulus to demand in the run-up to an election, and are subsequently obliged to impose restrictions. On the other hand, the same factors which, other things equal, make for a slower rate of growth, namely, heavy taxation and regulation and a large public sector, are also likely to be conducive to greater stability in the rate of growth.

Unemployment

If the theory of economic growth propounded in the previous section is accepted, then most unemployment can be understood as arising from a mismatch between the characteristics of the jobs destroyed and those created.

A classical explanation of unemployment might therefore run along the following lines: the rate of change in developed market economies has been increasing since the War. Within the last decade there has been an apparent acceleration in the rate of deployment of new technologies, while reductions in barriers to trade, deregulation and the extension of the market economy into the public sector have all contributed to more rapidly changing patterns of production and trade within and between economies. But the introduction of new goods and services as well as new processes has rendered redundant old goods and old processes. The pace of creative destruction has accelerated.

In these circumstances it is not surprising that at any period of time more people will be between jobs. The new jobs which are created will only by chance be in the same locations, in the same industries, in the same numbers and for workers with the same skills and aptitudes as those which have been lost. This has been traditionally known as the problem of labour mobility.

What is the remedy? One answer is that the problem is due to inflexible labour markets, and that if such markets were unfettered by removing tax and benefit disincentives to work, as well as such regulatory barriers as minimum wage laws, then the problem would resolve itself. A comparison of the experience of the United States and Europe in the last 20 years is often invoked in support of this argument. While the rate of economic growth in the two areas over this period has been similar, the United States has created many more jobs. Europe, on the other hand, has enjoyed a higher growth of average real wages, apparently at the expense of higher levels of unemployment than in the United States.

Macro-economic theory has always taken it for granted that both labour and capital could migrate from old jobs to new ones more or less costlessly. With capital, this is no longer the case, if ever it were true. Technical progress, and increasing specialisation over time, has meant that capital equipment has become ever more specific and durable, and hence less easily transferable. Upon being made redundant, the capital invested in a marginally profitable steel works, for instance, does not migrate to another industry: most of its value is destroyed. While formerly swords and ploughshares could both be turned out by a blacksmith working with an anvil, today it is more difficult to change the production lines required to assemble aircraft into production lines for making computer games.

Just as barriers to capital mobility have grown over time so, too, have barriers to labour mobility. Retraining can only overcome skill barriers; many aptitudes are not transferable. And there remain social, psychological and political barriers to inter-regional migration. Nevertheless, it is clear that if full employment policies are to succeed, they must facilitate as far as possible the adaptability of workers from old to new jobs. This process will be assisted by the reduction of disincentives to new employment, for instance by shifting taxes from employment to consumption and by shifting subsidies from unemployment to the search for, and acceptance of, new employment.

Money

For the classical economist, the supply of and demand for money should be determined by competitive market forces. As in the case of any other commodity, no state authority could possibly have the information with which to balance supply and demand as effectively as does the market.

From this point of view, the aggregate quantity of money is a variable of no policy significance, indeed of no special significance at all. Since bank liabilities are held willingly by the public, how much of them, in total, the banks have created is of no particular interest. The whole question of the 'moneyness' of different types of assets is therefore irrelevant. The objective of monetary policy in the classical view is to achieve price stability, an objective desirable both from the point of view of minimising the fluctuations of the business cycle in the medium term, and providing an environment conducive to growth in the long term.

Up to the First World War, price stability was in theory assured by the convertibility of money into gold. In practice, price stability was only assured so long as gold itself enjoyed a stable value in terms of other commodities. Following the First World War, this was no longer the case, and the era of 'managed money', in which central banks tried to achieve price stability by attempting to control the aggregate quantity of money, was ushered in.

Thanks, however, to financial innovation and the increasing freedom to move financial capital between monetary régimes, market forces today exercise increasing influence over the supply of money, but without the 'anchor' of convertibility which previously existed. This raises questions of stability.

Minsky, for example, argues that changes in the *quality* of privately issued monetary liabilities play an important part in the business cycle.[8] In contrast to the macro-economic view of money as a single inelastically supplied liability with known and constant properties, Minsky sees a spectrum of financial assets, elastically supplied, and with unknown and changing properties; as the economy evolves, new liabilities are invented. In the course of the business cycle, the quality of liabilities deteriorates as firms face difficulty in meeting their commitments and financing new outlays.

Hayek's Competing Currencies

Amongst those who adopt the classical view that the quantity of money supplied should be determined by market forces, two recent attempts to address the issue of stability stand out.

---

[8] H. Minsky, *Inflation, Recession and Economic Policy*, Brighton: Wheatsheaf Books, 1982.

Hayek[9] argued that if individual commercial banks had restored to them the freedom to issue their own currencies, and if restrictions on their ability to make loans and to accept deposits were at the same time abolished, competition between currencies would favour that currency most likely to maintain its value. In other words, people could be expected to prefer to hold a currency in whose future value, in terms of other commodities, they had grounds for confidence.

A somewhat analogous argument was advanced by the Treasury some years ago when it was attempting, on behalf of the Government, to deflect the proposal for a Single European Currency. The Treasury counter-proposed there should instead be a system of competing national currencies. From this system, a single currency might indeed evolve, but if it did, it would only be as a result of the wishes of the holders of that currency. So long as the right to issue competing currencies was retained, any future attempt at the political manipulation of the single currency would be restrained.

Supporters of Hayek's view of the stability of a completely deregulated banking system point to historical experience, notably that of the Scottish banking system in the one hundred years before the Bank Charter Act of 1844 which effectively transferred the monopoly of the note issue to the Bank of England.[10] However, Glasner points out that during this period the notes issued by the Scottish banks were always convertible into gold. Glasner himself takes the view that price stability within the contemporary monetary system can be guaranteed only by convertibility into a real asset. He proposes therefore that commercial banks should have the right to convert their currencies into a state-sponsored monetary unit convertible into gold at a variable rate designed to stabilise the general price level.[11]

Whatever the merits of this particular proposal, it seems clear that the anomaly of attempted state control of the money supply may not last much longer. With the existing instruments of monetary policy being undermined by the

9 Hayek (1990), *op.cit.*; see also Hayek's *Choice in Currency: A Way to Stop Inflation*, IEA Occasional Paper No.48, London: Institute of Economic Affairs, 1976.

10 M. Fry, *Banking Deregulation*, Hume Paper No.1, Edinburgh: The David Hume Institute, 1985.

11 Glasner, *op.cit.*, p.247.

continuing evolution of a quasi-competitive monetary system, the pretensions to knowledge of central bankers are embarrassingly exposed. While the current tendency towards central bank independence makes it more difficult for elected politicians to tamper with the currency, it also means that central bankers will no longer be able to blame politicians for policy failures. If, as seems likely, the present arrangements are unable to maintain long-term price stability, the failure of macro-economic monetary policy will be complete.

Forecasting

As we saw in Section III (subsection entitled 'Macro-economic Models', above, p.27), it is not possible, in general, to forecast the specific values of particular prices and quantities at some future date. This is so because we do not possess a sufficient understanding of the processes involved in determining these values; even if we did, the forecaster would still lack the necessary information to make the forecast because that information is widely disseminated amongst market participants.

Recent work in the study of non-linear dynamics,[12] however, lends support to Hayek's contention that what he called 'pattern predictions' are possible in economics – that is, the general character rather than the detail of the consequences which flow from the application of economic theories can be predicted. Such theories are still empirically testable since 'the order implies the existence of certain relationships between the elements, and the actual presence or absence of such relationships can be ascertained'.[13]

Amongst such pattern predictions might be that intensification of competition within an industry will lead, over time, to a reduction in the number of participating firms and a lowering of the average cost of production. It is possible for observers to discern trends in the medium-term evolution of a particular economy, by applying the appropriate principles of economic theory in conjunction with their subjective judgement. Some such judgements will prove to be correct,

---

[12] J. Gleick, *Chaos: Making A New Science*, London: Penguin Books, 1987, and Parker & Stacey, *op.cit.*

[13] F.A. Hayek, *Studies in Philosophy, Politics and Economics*, London: Routledge & Kegan Paul, 1967, p.261.

others will prove to be wrong. And even those trends which are correctly discerned may be arrested or reversed at any time.

Pattern predictions may form the basis for recommending policies that may be applied to adjust the future course of an economic system in some desired way. An obvious contemporary example is the attempt which is being made to alter the institutions of the economic systems of the former Soviet Union, and of other formerly planned economies throughout the world, in the direction of a tolerably functioning market economy. It should be noted that, within a broad institutional environment of the kind proposed by Adam Smith, *viz.* '... peace, easy taxes and a tolerable administration of justice ...', a market economy, untrammelled by excessive regulation, will evolve its own internal institutions. This is in contrast to the institutions of a socialist economy which have to be self-consciously 'built'.

Pattern predictions in this context require an understanding of the true nature of the market process as a discovery mechanism, the importance of entrepreneurship in a context of uncertainty, and the importance of a framework of appropriate institutions. Equally important, but more difficult to achieve, is a simultaneous appreciation of the particular historical and societal context within which such changes are to take place. Unlike modern macro-economic theory which locates events in a mechanistic process, the classical approach recognises that all events take place in an historical process which is non-deterministic and irreversible, and in which unique factors can have a decisive influence.

It is this approach of which Baumol complains that 'it does not form a deterministic model which grinds out history with an inexorability which permits us to predict it'.[14]

Baumol contrasts this early classical approach unfavourably with the approach of the later classical school (for example, Ricardo, James Mill, McCulloch and Senior), from whose work he synthesised a model predicting 'inexorably' the arrival of the stationary state in England.

Some might regard this model as a forerunner of macro-economics, since it is based on a number of empirical generalisations about the behaviour of aggregates. On the

---

[14] Baumol, *op.cit.*, p.35.

other hand, its predictions may be classed as pattern predictions, since all that is predicted is the distributional share of the aggregate factors of production at the time of arrival of the stationary state, an event for which no specific date is forecast.

VI. IMPLICATIONS OF THE ALTERNATIVE APPROACH

Implications for Government Policy

If macro-economic theory is to be abandoned, how are the objectives of stabilisation policy to be achieved? To take first the case of price stability, how can governments prevent inflationary pressures from building up without at the same time stifling growth of output?

We have argued above (in Section IV, subsection entitled 'The "New" Macro-economics', above, p.36) that monetary policy in the macro-economic sense is undesirable, and that the objective of price stability would be better served by the deregulation of banking. This may prove too radical an agenda even for a Government apparently committed to the principles of market liberalisation.

If that is the case, then, in our present state of knowledge, economists have little else in the way of scientific advice to offer government on monetary policy. Before being able to offer any such advice, it would be necessary to carry out detailed research into the transmission mechanisms of both monetary and fiscal policy. If such research is to be fruitful, it must be willing to admit a wider range of factors, notably institutional and psychological influences, than those brought into conventional macro-economic analysis. A successful approach is likely to be more disaggregated, and if a theory is to be constructed which will be helpful in policy, it must be formulated in a less mechanistic way than that which has characterised macro-economic theory hitherto. The difficulties of research in this area should not be underestimated. In particular, it should be recognised that the phenomena under investigation are subject to continuous qualitative as well as quantitative change.

Fluctuations in Output

What about economy-wide fluctuations in output? Can government do nothing about those?

[63]

A classical perspective recognises that economic growth in a market economy takes place through a succession of cumulative and self-reinforcing changes which are cyclical in nature. The 'remedial' recession follows inexorably from the excesses of the preceding boom. In contemporary circumstances, the result for most developed market economies is usually a fairly mild cycle about which little can be done, or perhaps even needs to be done.

Governments themselves are often responsible for exacerbating fluctuations with mistaken policies. This is not only a question of governments failing to predict correctly the values of some macro-economic variables, although in the post-war period examples of destabilising counter-cyclical policies can be found. It is also a question of adding artificial rigidities into the economic system. The history of the UK in the EMS from the Autumn of 1990 to the Autumn of 1992 provides an illustration of this point. And, of course, the political business cycle is due to government.

Nevertheless, the fact that governments in the developed market economies account for some 40 per cent of total economic activity acts as a stabilising influence. In general, the less regulated is the economy, the smaller the proportion of government activity, the more unfettered the competition, and the more open the markets, then the greater the degree of instability which may be expected.

More severe endogenous disturbances cannot be ruled out in future. One possible threat to the stability of the developed market economies at the present time comes from the financial services sector. A speculative bubble based on derivative financial instruments could conceivably draw liquidity suddenly and on a substantial scale out of the commercial banking system. Although one would not expect the monetary authorities to stand idly by, as they did during the Great Depression, it cannot be assumed that they would be able to judge correctly the appropriate adjustment required. Following the October 1987 stock exchange crash, the Federal Reserve made clear their willingness to inject the necessary liquidity into the US banking system. In the UK, the Government's response was to reduce interest rates. These actions, which appeared acceptable at the time, may have contributed to the inflationary pressures of 1988-90.

Other fluctuations may be attributed to external shocks. It is one of the curiosities of historical experience that developed market economies have sometimes absorbed large external shocks successfully, while on other occasions they seem to have reacted strongly to modest shocks. This suggests that the response mechanism is more important than the degree of severity of the external shock, and that monetary institutions and monetary organisation play a decisive rôle in the response mechanism. One may imagine what havoc the 1973-74 oil price shock would have wrought if the Bretton Woods system of fixed exchange rates had still remained in place.

Both politicians and economists must also learn a lesson in modesty: we need to understand before we can pretend to control. In particular, it has to be generally recognised that governments do not yet have it within their power to deliver sustained growth *and* price stability (at least not without making significant institutional changes). One cannot rule out that they will one day stumble across a means of doing so, but that day has yet to arrive. Governments can therefore only to a limited extent be held accountable for the short-term performance of a developed market economy. Except in the case of obvious mistakes, they should receive neither credit nor blame for this performance.

Implications For Business

For most businessmen, the connection between macro-economic variables and the variables with which they themselves are immediately concerned is tenuous. The prospects of one company may be affected by particular factors such as the values of certain interest rates or of certain exchange rates, which will be different from other factors influencing other companies. Even apparently economy-wide fluctuations in output and income have markedly different consequences for different industries. Accordingly, macro-economics may not be of great interest to the business community in general.

Within the financial services sector, however, there is a particular interest in the values of certain macro-economic variables. For participants in the bond and equity markets, an ability to predict values of the short-term rate of interest and the rate of inflation is important. Here, traders expect to make money by correctly anticipating movements in these variables. Success in this respect depends on two factors:

o A judgement of how the markets concerned will respond to movements in the short-term interest rate and in the rate of inflation; and

o An accurate prediction of these two variables.

The first is a subjective factor which varies from one individual trader to another. The interest rate and the rate of inflation are among the variables most commonly forecast by macro-economic models which have been no more successful in producing adequate forecasts for the rate of inflation than for any other macro-economic variable; such forecasts therefore remain a matter of individual subjective judgement. And that judgement must encompass a wider range of factors than the purely quantitative or even the purely economic. For example, to have forecast correctly the rate of inflation in Germany following unification would have required making the political judgement that the German authorities would not finance unification by increased taxation.

In developed market economies the short-term rate of interest is wholly policy-determined, and therefore what is required is a political judgement when, and in which direction, the authorities will move.

Consequently, success in financial market forecasting depends entirely on subjective judgement which may usually be associated with experience of the markets concerned. It cannot be attributed to macro-economic modelling; those City analysts who claim to base their monthly or quarterly forecasts on macro-economic models are doing themselves and their clients a disservice.

Most businessmen would, of course, like to know the future prices of the goods and services they produce or trade or on which their business may depend. With this knowledge, few would fail to be successful. It is therefore understandable that there should be a continuing demand for such information, but only the ill-informed will give credence to forecasts produced by macro-economic models.

For those businessmen who must take major decisions, the most effective way of coping with uncertainty is to undertake some form or other of risk management. This may extend to buying risk contracts in the market. For the great majority whose commercial risks are less well-defined, there is the possibility of adopting contingency planning techniques.

One such technique which has been developed in the past two decades is known as scenario planning. This approach starts from the premise that the future is unknowable in detail, and that therefore attempts at the prediction or forecasting of specific economic events are bound to fail. Instead, what is prepared is a series of alternative internally consistent descriptions of the future – the scenarios. Each scenario describes a sequence of possible future events, some of which may be expected to have an influence on the future performance of the business concerned, through factors which are both important and uncertain. These critical factors will usually differ from one company to another.

Once the scenarios have been prepared, a proposed investment decision can be tested for robustness against each scenario in turn. Other things equal, that strategy may be preferred which performs well under most scenarios. For example, suppose a decision is to be made by a firm whether to invest a large amount of capital in the acquisition of an asset in a new industry or a new country. If the decision looks good in only one of several scenarios, it must be classed as a high-risk venture.

It may be significant that the Central Planning Bureau of the Netherlands, an institution which pioneered macro-economic modelling and forecasting, now uses scenario planning techniques to analyse the medium and long-term future.[1]

Implications for Academic Teaching and Research

Introduction

Disquiet about the teaching of economics in universities has been growing in recent years. In 1988 the American Economic Association set up a Commission on graduate training which reported in 1991.[2] The Commission's major concern was the

---

[1] See Central Planning Bureau of the Netherlands, *Scanning The Future*, The Hague: SUD, 1992. For an excellent introduction to scenario planning see P. Schwartz, *The Art of the Long View*, London: Century Business, 1992.

[2] Anne Krueger *et.al.*, 'Report of the Commission on Graduate Education in Economics', *Journal of Economic Literature*, Vol.29, September 1991, pp.1,035-53.

extent to which graduate education in economics had become too far removed from actual economic problems, so that economists were being turned out who were skilled in technique but innocent of real economic issues.

Others who have surveyed student opinion report that graduate students do not like the current preoccupation with techniques; they want more ideas, more policy relevance, more discussion of the fundamental assumptions, and more serious consideration of alternative approaches. 'Many students enter graduate school with lofty ideals, and it is sad to see those crushed.'[3]

More recently, a number of practising economists have expressed their dissatisfaction with the state of current teaching and research. Mayer distinguishes between formalist techniques and what he calls empirical science theory, and suggests a twin-track approach in which the latter is accorded the same prestige within the profession as the former now enjoys.[4] Ormerod is dismissive of orthodox competitive equilibrium analysis, but offers no very clear alternative in its place.[5] At the same time, there has been a resurgence of interest in evolutionary perspectives and in institutional economics.[6]

A broader curriculum for the teaching of economics can be built on the three pillars suggested by Schumpeter, namely, Economic Theory, Economic History and Statistics.[7]

Economic Theory

So far as the theory of value, or micro-economic theory is concerned, there is still a place at the elementary level for the neo-classical theory of value. Few economists would wish to dispense with the explanatory power of simple supply and demand analysis. For more advanced micro-economic theory, the introduction of uncertainty, subjectivism, and the

---

[3] A. Klamer and D. Colander, *The Making of an Economist*, Boulder, Col:Westview Press, 1990, p.184.

[4] T. Mayer, *Truth versus Precision in Economics*, Aldershot: Edward Edgar, 1993.

[5] P. Ormerod, *The Death of Economics*, London: Faber and Faber, 1994.

[6] See, for example, H. Hanusch (ed.), *Evolutionary Economics*, Cambridge: Cambridge University Press, 1988, and Hodgson, *op.cit.*

[7] J.A. Schumpeter, *History of Economic Analysis*, New York: Oxford University Press, 1954, Ch.2.

entrepreneurial nature of human behaviour moves us into the realm of Austrian economics. The interdependence of all the social sciences implicit in the title *Human Action* which von Mises gave to his great work of economic theory ought to be recognised in teaching.

The theory of economic growth and business cycles should stress the institutional and evolutionary elements in these topics, in contrast to the optimisation and institution-free perspectives which dominate at the present time. Increasing the importance of growth in the curriculum would represent a return to the classical tradition, and at the same time can be related to Economic History, the second pillar of the curriculum. Monetary theory should move away from its dependence on the quantity theory, towards a greater understanding of its institutional context. In summary, what is required in economic theory is a broadening of the curriculum, introducing a richer and wider content at the expense of current narrow formalism. The work of such cognate disciplines as management theory, history and political science should no longer be ignored.

One possible avenue for teaching theory at the undergraduate level which for too long has been neglected is the history of economic thought. This approach introduces students to a wide range of ideas, a discussion of fundamental assumptions, and a more serious consideration of alternative approaches.[8]

There would seem to be two main problems with the formalism that characterises the present academic curriculum for teaching economics. First, it has led to an excessive refinement of analysis, a process whereby precision has been achieved at the cost of accuracy and the elimination of some of the most valuable variables. Secondly, as Mayer points out, economists often draw policy conclusions from models that, for reasons of tractability, deal only with a part of the problem. That failing has a long tradition in economics. Schumpeter called it 'the Ricardian Vice'.[9]

---

[8] An indication of the malign consequences of the post-war neglect of the history of economic thought is to be found in the index to Ormerod's recent book, where Jeffrey Sachs is mentioned but not Schumpeter, and Jevons and Walras are but not Menger.

[9] Schumpeter (1954), *op.cit.*, p.473.

There are at least three reasons why economic history should be a required subject for study by everyone who aspires to become a professional economist.

First, economic history is the source of all the factual information upon which the science of economics depends. It is scarcely desirable to rely upon this information as the basis of study without some understanding of how it has been arrived at; some understanding of the process of historical interpretation is required. This proposition is equally true whether one is thinking of quantitative or qualitative information.

Second, the study of economic history reveals the interaction of economic with non-economic factors. It demonstrates the frequent importance of non-economic factors influencing economic events.

Third, the study of economic history shows that economic events are composed of both unique and general elements. Economic theory teaches one to look exclusively for general causes of economic phenomena. But history shows that unique events (such as German re-unification) can often be decisive in determining movements in the values of important economic variables (European interest rates).

Mayer suggests that it may be useful to acquaint students with a broader range of experience, such as observing decision-making processes and using polling data.[10] The important rôle that some economists see for experimental economics, or for inter-disciplinary work, or for analysing irrational behaviour suggests that we should broaden the range of analytical tools that we teach. In general, greater use should be made of case study material as a means of teaching students how to apply economic theories to practical problems and to illustrate the rôle played by a wide range of factors in economic affairs.

Statistics

Most contemporary programmes leading to economics degrees, whether at undergraduate or postgraduate level, require their students to take at least one elementary course in

---

[10] Mayer, *op.cit.,* p.162.

quantitative methods. The syllabus for such a course consists largely of applied statistics – the more or less mechanistic application of standard formulae to data which have been derived from official statistical publications. Despite the periodic revision of such statistical series as GDP, or the various alternative measures of the money supply, there remains an uncritical attitude among academics towards statistics produced by official agencies. Too often, graduate students can complete their macro-economic courses without finding out that the data they use are subject to substantial and continuing revisions.

It would be preferable if the time at present devoted to teaching applied statistics and econometrics were instead devoted to teaching (a) the fundamental principles of statistical theory, and (b) the interpretation of statistical data according to these principles. Such a proposal has two practical objectives. First, to teach the student how to analyse quantitative evidence. Every modern society is bombarded by an ever-increasing volume of data. It is not only the official statistical agencies which are responsible for the flow of doubtful 'facts'; also at work are large private corporations and political interest groups of every persuasion. Secondly, such data need to be screened not only for their reliability but also for the inferences, if any, which can be drawn from them.

In summary, the principles of statistical theory should be taught in place of econometrics. Emphasis should be placed on the evaluation and interpretation of data.

Macro-economics in the Curriculum

Macro-economics can perhaps be defended on the grounds that it provides an acceptable first approximation to the truth, a kind of short-hand or back-of-the-envelope approach to economics. It can serve for descriptive rather than analytical purposes. As such, it is used by politicians or journalists.[11] However, as we have argued in this paper, aggregate concepts stand in the way of clear thinking about the economy. For the reasons stated, macro-economic theory is fundamentally

---

[11] Although even this function can be dangerous, as the weight placed upon the so-called Maastricht conditions illustrates. The nonsensical nature of these conditions is demonstrated by Krugman in his *Peddling Prosperity*, New York: Norton, 1994, pp. 190-91.

inadequate, and, when applied, gives conclusions which are misleading in practice. It should therefore be avoided if possible by economists practising in business or in the Civil Service, and eschewed at all costs by theoretical economists. If it is to retain any place at all in the teaching curriculum, it might appear in the history of economic thought. In this *Hobart Paper* I hope I have demonstrated that there is no need for it anywhere else.

Macro-economics and Micro-economics

It may be asked whether the foregoing criticisms of excessive formalism in the current curriculum do not apply equally to micro-economics. It is true there are examples of excessive refinement to be found in all branches of the current curriculum. Just as the so-called New Classical macro-economics (which may be new, but is certainly not classical) can be seen as the result of excessive refinement in macro-economic theory, so the Arrow-Debreu model of competitive general economic equilibrium can be seen as the result of excessive refinement in the area of micro-economics.

However, there are at least three reasons why the case against neo-classical micro-economic theory is less strong. *First*, as suggested above, few economists of any shade of opinion within the profession would doubt the value of elementary supply and demand analysis. The concept of equilibrium seems less inappropriate in the context of the individual decision unit than in the context of the economy as a whole. It is only the excessive refinement of micro-economic theory which has led to difficulties. But even the most elementary macro-economic theory has the fundamental flaws discussed in Section IV.

Second, macro-economics is undermined by the existence of uncertainty and unfulfilled expectations, to a greater extent than is micro-economic theory.[12] Furthermore, there appears to be less disagreement amongst economists on micro-economic policy questions. Whilst economists still differ on

---

[12] 'When errors, ignorance and uncertainty about expectations are taken to be serious, then there are few firm and reliable general assumptions on which to build valid general theories of employment, interest and money.' (T.W. Hutchison, *The Limits of General Theories in Macro-economics*, Washington DC: American Enterprise Institute, 1980.

such issues of public policy as protection of the environment or the regulation of industry, these differences are less likely to spring from differences about fundamental theory than is the case with macro-economics.

Third, micro-economics does not suffer from the assumption that the value of an aggregate is more important than its composition.

Giving up the Macro-economic Paradigm

Those academic readers who are persuaded by the argument of this paper will be faced with the psychologically difficult task of abandoning a paradigm which has occupied a prominent part of their professional lifetime. Many will understandably be loath to do so. A few may respond by reaffirming their belief in macro-economics still more fervently.

Outside the academic community, support is already ebbing away. Amongst wider informed opinion, there is little respect remaining for macro-economic policy, and thus for the reasoning which lies behind it. The appointment of the unorthodox Laura d'Andrea Tyson, a Berkeley Professor, rather than a macro-economist as Chairwoman of President Clinton's Council of Economic Advisers was significant.[13] In the United Kingdom, it is to merchant bankers rather than to economists that the Government has turned for advice on the privatisation of the great public utilities – telecommunications, gas, water, electricity and the railways. When they need advice, business corporations and government departments are nowadays more likely to turn to management consultants than to economic consultants.

As Minford has observed about the usefulness of macro-economic theory, 'ultimately, as with other professional activities, it is the end user in the market who must make up

---

[13] Commenting on this appointment, the Washington correspondent of the *Financial Times* wrote: '... Mr Clinton is signalling his exasperation with the economics profession which he feels has shed little light on the long-run forces undermining US productivity growth and living standards ... It worships mathematical technique but pays little attention to the real world ... It has lost relevance by trying to pretend that economics is a "hard science" totally divorced from such related subjects as politics, psychology and sociology. It has lost its ability to communicate with the laity.' (Michael Prowse, 'A Wake Up Call from Laura Tyson', *Financial Times*, 18 January 1993.)

his mind how to use the talents at his disposal'.[14] The market has given its verdict.

As market forces increasingly determine the allocation of resources among and within universities, then, unless changes to the curriculum are made, we shall find that enrolment and funding will gradually move away from Departments of Economics towards Departments of Business Studies or even to Business Schools, which may be tempted to set up their own courses or even departments of 'Applied Economics'.

It would be a tragedy if this were to happen. What is not required is the substitution of applied economics for theoretical economics. That has always been a false antithesis. What is required is the abandonment of macro-economics, which is fundamentally theoretically flawed and epitomises the narrow formalism which has characterised the economics curriculum in recent years, and its replacement by a return to the classical tradition in economic theory.

---

[14] P. Minford, 'Comment', in T. Mayer and F. Spinelli (eds.), *Macro-economics and Macro-economic Policy Issues,* Aldershot: Avebury, 1991, p.264.

VII. SUMMARY AND CONCLUSIONS

1. The distinguishing feature of developed market economies is incessant qualitative change. New consumer and capital goods, and new methods of production and distribution, are continuously being created and old ones destroyed.

2. Macro-economics is a way of looking at economic activity in terms of aggregates and averages. As such, it obscures rather than assists an understanding of the essential features of economic activity in a market economy.

3. Macro-economics is theoretically flawed because it makes unwarranted assertions about the stability of empirical relationships between aggregates, assumes their unchanging composition, abstracts from essential elements of economic activity, and uses concepts out of context. Recent developments in macro-economic theory have not addressed these defects, rather they have aggravated them.

4. In general, it is impossible to predict to what extent an increase in aggregate demand will be reflected in price rises and to what extent in output increases. In order to know what significance to attach to a numerical value for any aggregate, one has to disaggregate.

5. Aggregate concepts such as the NAIRU, the quantity of money, the output gap and competitiveness are all misleading, and have contributed to the implementation of unsuccessful and sometimes harmful policies.

6. Almost 20 years since it was publicly acknowledged that a government could not spend its way out of a recession, it has been discovered that the fine tuning of bank lending does not work either. In the UK the operation of monetary policy has been uncoupled from macro-economic theory.

7. The cycle is an intrinsic part of the deregulated developed market economy and one cannot have the benefits of growth without it.

8. Repeated surveys have shown the complete failure of all attempts at short-term forecasting using macro-economic models. Only pattern predictions are possible.

9. Macro-economic theory is a dead end in the history of economic thought. The way forward is to return to the classical tradition which emphasises the importance of uncertainty, innovation, entrepreneurship and institutional evolution, and avoids spurious precision. This approach has quite different policy implications.

10. Policies to approach full employment must facilitate the adaptation of workers from old jobs to new jobs. This process will be assisted by shifting taxes from employment to consumption and by shifting subsidies from unemployment to the search for, and acceptance of, new employment.

QUESTIONS FOR DISCUSSION

1. What are the principal assumptions underlying macro economic theory? What are the implications of these assumptions?

2. Is it appropriate to apply the concept of equilibrium to the whole of an economy?

3. 'The output gap', 'the quantity of money' and (national) competitiveness are all phrases in common use. Do they have any theoretical basis?

4. Why should we not leave monetary policy to be determined by central bankers?

5. Why do macro economic forecasts have such a consistent record of failure?

6. Can macro economic theory throw any light on the causes of the current levels of unemployment in European countries?

7. Comment on the exclusion of innovation, entrepreneurship and other institutional elements from macro economic analysis.

8. Assess the validity of the convergence criteria for progress towards monetary union laid down in the Maastricht Treaty.

9. Why has macro economics been unable to explain the US productivity slowdown which began in 1973?

10. Why is a growing economy unlikely ever to be in 'equilibrium'?

FURTHER READING

General

Lachmann, L.M., *Macro economic Thinking and the Market Economy*, Hobart Paper No.56, London: Institute of Economic Affairs, 1973.

Schumpeter, J.A., *History of Economic Analysis*, New York: Oxford University Press, 1954.

Hayek, F.A., *Studies in Philosophy, Politics and Economics*, London: Routledge & Kegan Paul, 1967.

Hayek, F.A., *New Studies in Philosophy, Politics and Economics and the History of Ideas*, London: Routledge & Kegan Paul, 1978.

Gordon, R.A., '*Rigor and Relevance in a Changing Institutional Setting*', American Economic Review, Vol.60, No.1, March 1976.

Kirzner, I.M., *Competition and Entrepreneurship*, Chicago: Chicago University Press, 1973.

Krugman, P., *Peddling Prosperity*, New York: W.W. Norton, 1994.

Mayer, T., *Truth versus Precision in Economics*, Aldershot: Edward Elgar, 1993.

Drucker, P.F., *Post Capitalist Society*, Oxford: Butterworth Heinemann, 1993.

Growth

Schumpeter, J.A., *The Theory of Economic Development*, Cambridge, Mass.: Harvard University Press, 1934.

Rosenberg, N., *Exploring the Black Box: Technology, Economics and History*, Cambridge: Cambridge University Press, 1994.

Young, Allyn, 'Increasing Returns and Economic Progress', *Economic Journal*, 1928, pp.529 42.

Boulding, K.E., *Evolutionary Economics*, London: Sage, 1981.

Money

Hayek, F.A., *The Denationalisation of Money*, Hobart Paper No.70, 1st Edn., 1976, 3rd Edn., 1990, London: Institute of Economic Affairs.

Glasner, D., *Free Banking and Monetary Reform*, Cambridge: Cambridge University Press, 1989.

Minsky, H.P., *Inflation, Recession and Economic Policy*, Brighton: Wheatsheaf Books, 1982.

Forecasting

Streissler, E.W., *Pitfalls in Econometric Forecasting*, Research Monograph No.23, London: Institute of Economic Affairs, 1970.

Schwartz, P., *The Art of the Long View*, London: Century Business, 1992.